A Boring Way to Get Rich

A Boring Way to Get Rich

The Beginner's Guide to Mutual Funds

Dhirendra Kumar

JUGGERNAUT BOOKS
C-I-128, First Floor, Sangam Vihar, Near Holi Chowk,
New Delhi 110080, India

First published by Juggernaut Books 2023

Copyright © Dhirendra Kumar 2023

10 9 8 7 6 5 4 3 2 1

P-ISBN: 9789353451776
E-ISBN: 9789353451745

The views and opinions expressed in this book are the author's own. The facts contained herein were reported to be true as on the date of publication by the author to the publishers of the book, and the publishers are not in any way liable for their accuracy or veracity.

All rights reserved. No part of this publication may be reproduced, transmitted, or stored in a retrieval system in any form or by any means without the written permission of the publisher.

Typeset in Adobe Caslon Pro by R. Ajith Kumar, Noida

Printed at Thomson Press India Ltd

Contents

The Value Research Story — vii
Preface — xiii

Introduction: Compounding and Inflation — 1

1. Your Needs — 13
2. Risk, Reward and Liquidity — 19
3. Asset Allocation — 29
4. Understanding Your Needs — 39
5. What Are Mutual Funds? — 45
6. Systematic Investment — 59
7. Portfolios and How to Build Them — 65
8. Types of Funds and Their Uses — 75
9. Investing for Growth: Model Portfolios — 89
10. Using Debt Funds to Invest for Income — 103
11. Long-Term Planning for Retirement — 119

12.	Exchange-Traded Funds, Insurance and Unit-Linked Insurance Plans	139
13.	Tax Treatments of Investments	149
14.	Picking a Fund: What to Look For	157
15.	How to Do It: The Nuts and Bolts	169

Afterword	179
Acknowledgements	183
A Note on the Author	185

The Value Research Story

It began with a simple clip file – a physical folder secured with a clip. That file held my pioneering set of reports on Public Sector Undertakings (PSUs), researched, compiled and written freshly after graduating from the College of Business Studies in 1990 at the age of 20. It was an exciting time for someone like me – the dawn of India's economic reforms. Amongst many radical changes, PSU disinvestments too were first proposed. I managed to have these reports published in *The Economic Times*, marking the humble beginnings of Value Research.

It's hard to imagine for the new generation, but in the years before the internet became widely available in India, newspapers and magazines were the only sources of regular investment data. However, they didn't carry anything at all on mutual funds. So, I collaborated with *The Economic Times* in 1993 to launch India's first mutual fund scorecard. This printed database continued to be published weekly in the paper for more than a decade; in a way, it was the precursor to our website.

In 1993, I also created and published India's first fund ratings in *Business Today* magazine, launching the rating system that, 30 years later, is still India's most trusted home-grown fund rating service. From the beginning, Value Research earned credibility because my analysis was objective and independent and not tied to any fund house or brokerage. No matter what our readers bought and through whatever channel, Value Research wouldn't stand to gain. Essentially, we were a super-specialized media operation.

Over the next few years, Value Research's reach in the media expanded vastly with publications like *The Times of India*, *The Economic Times*, *Business Standard*, *Deccan Chronicle*, *The Telegraph*, *Amar Ujala Karobar*, *The Financial Express* and *Eenadu* beginning to carry mutual fund data and analysis from Value Research. Even Bloomberg, the global authority on financial data, started using Value Research data as part of its service.

When the internet came along, I was an early adopter. It was a must! Every wannabe financial portal approached Value Research for mutual fund data and analysis during the dot-com boom. Not only did this solidify our reputation as India's most accurate and reliable source of mutual fund data, it more or less pushed me to launch our own portal, as readers who came across our analysis online at other portals started to contact us directly.

This is how we grew into India's foremost independent investment research firm. Value Research now has a team of well over 100 people, offering data, analysis and opinion on stocks, mutual funds and fixed-income investments through our website, valueresearchonline.com, our periodicals, *Mutual Fund Insight* and *Wealth Insight*, and through many other products and services.

We continue to be the most trusted source of information on mutual funds and stocks for millions of investors, advisors, media companies and even the fund houses themselves. Much of our data and analysis is freely available.

Apart from broad and deep coverage of the mutual fund industry, we also offer free portfolio selection and analysis tools. In addition, we offer premium services and subscriptions to our magazines. Our affiliate, Independent Advisors Private Limited, offers investment advisory services. As an investment advisor registered with the Securities and Exchange Board of India (SEBI), Independent Advisors provides financial advice and transaction services. Independent Advisors runs Value Research Stock Advisor, a research-driven stock recommendation service which grew out of my more than 30 years of experience in equity research.

Value Research Online was officially launched in 2001 and rapidly became India's most popular online source of mutual fund data for investors. Two decades later, it's still comfortably holding that position. Every month, more than a million people visit the site, and our subscription base includes many who have been visiting the website since its inception. We continue to offer data and advice independently.

In 2002 and 2006, we launched two monthly magazines – *Mutual Fund Insight*, which covers mutual funds, and *Wealth Insight*, which covers equity investments. Published in association with ICICIdirect, *Wealth Insight* instantly became India's largest equity investment publication. Note that the magazine remained independent – while ICICIdirect offered it to their clients, we did not push ICICIdirect services or stand to make money from the trades made by ICICIdirect clients.

In 2017, we launched the stock advisory service, Value Research Stock Advisor, to help investors pick good companies for the long term. This remains a purely advisory model. Stock Advisor suggests investments, and it will help you track your portfolio. You can buy the stocks from any brokerage of your choice in any quantity you choose.

In 2019, we introduced the online data and analysis toolset Value Research Analytics Pro. This is a more profound, authoritative research tool for mutual funds and is used extensively by financial advisors and researchers.

In 2020, we launched Value Research Premium. This premium service packs a whole warehouse of value-added features, from a portfolio planner to goal-oriented fund categories. It could be your one-stop destination to build a robust investment portfolio.

We also offer a range of investment-related books and manuals to help you stay ahead in your investment game. My family and I privately hold the company. We've always been profitable and are entirely self-funded with no loans or investments from any other source. The Value Research team is a close-knit, lean, multi-disciplinary family of analysts, writers, technologists and support staff.

Headquartered in the NCR in our own facility and with a marketing and analytical presence in Mumbai, Chennai and Kolkata, our stellar team strives to deliver stellar products that positively impact millions of investors and empower them to invest wisely to achieve their financial goals.

Preface

This book is aimed at the reader who wants to learn the basics of investing. There are many ways to invest and create wealth, but this book focuses on mutual funds because they are the safest, easiest way to grow your savings. In the chapters that follow, you will learn how mutual funds work and how you can utilize them without having to deal with too much financial complexity and without spending too much time.

Being a beginner at something is not a handicap – it's actually an opportunity. At Value Research, we love to interact with newbie investors, and we're always happy to get questions and letters from them because these help us learn. Beginners tend to question the basics, the things that everyone with some experience believes to be settled truths. This is why even after two decades of thinking and writing about investing, I find that the best way to learn is to answer the questions of a beginner.

Having said that, this book is not really only for

beginners. It works just as well as a refresher for readers who know something about the subject. Remember, refreshers are really useful – my own experience bears this out. I've been analysing investments for more than two decades, but even now, sometimes there is a moment or two when I feel like a complete novice. I come across something – a new investment product, an article or blog post that mentions a new approach to or way of analysing something – and I realize that I don't really understand it. Then, I look for more information and sit back and think about whatever has puzzled me till I feel I've understood it. In many ways, this is the best part of doing what I do. It's a great feeling to learn something new, to have fresh knowledge or insights.

At Value Research, we get a lot of questions from investors every day on email and sometimes even through the post! These are questions from beginners as well as from people who have been investing for a while. Most often though, it's only the beginners who are looking for real answers. More experienced investors are often just looking for confirmation of what they already know. If what they know is useful, that's a good thing. But if it's not, if their ideas about investing are mistaken, harmful or misleading in any way, then they're much worse off than the beginners. This is probably true in all spheres of life – it's awfully hard to unlearn the wrong things. It really is better to be a beginner than to have the wrong ideas.

A little while ago, I came across a superb beginners' guide on investing. It's written by the cartoonist Scott Adams, the creator of the amazing Dilbert comic strip, which so brilliantly makes fun of office life. The 'book' is called *Everything You Need to Know about Personal Investing*. It is actually just one page in Adams' book *Dilbert and the Way of the Weasel*.

Here it is in its entirety:

- Make a will.
- Pay off your credit card balance.
- Get term life insurance if you have a family to support.
- Fund your company 401(k) to the maximum.
- Fund your IRA to the maximum.
- Buy a house if you want to live in a house and can afford it.
- Put six months' expenses in a money market account.
- Take whatever money is left over and invest 70 per cent in a stock index fund and 30 per cent in a bond fund through any discount brokerage company and never touch it till retirement.
- If any of this confuses you, or you have something special going on (retirement, college planning, tax issue), hire a fee-based financial planner, not one who charges a percentage of your folio.*

---

* Scott Adams, *Dilbert and the Way of the Weasel*, Boxtree, 2003, p. 178.

Adams said that he always wanted to write a book on personal finance. But by the time he had thought through everything, simplified the steps and taken them to their logical end, he only had these few sentences!

This is really sound advice. Of course, Adams writes not only for the American context but also for a reader who's fairly young and an employee. Thus, some of the advice is not directly applicable in India, and some may need to be tweaked for your specific age and circumstance. Here, for example, you replace the 401(k) and the individual retirement account with equivalents such as the Employees Provident Fund and the Public Provident Fund and other such investments available under section 80C of the Income Tax Act.

In this book, we focus on Adam's last bullet point – how to take your surplus savings and invest for the long-term using mutual funds as instruments. That's all you have to do, and your 'Dilbert Portfolio' will be up and running. It's really quite simple, and you'll understand the concepts perfectly by the time you are done reading this book.

Reading a book targeted at beginners inevitably raises the question: What's the next step? Is there an advanced book for those who want to know more? And perhaps a 'super-advanced' one after that?

Well, Value Research does offer a range of books and magazines that you might like to read, if you become really interested in investing. But you don't *need* any of them. What you learn from here, backed up with the data, information and analysis we offer on our free-to-access website, valueresearchonline.com, should be quite enough to ensure a lifetime of happy, successful, hassle-free and profitable investing.

And that's exactly what all of us at Value Research want for you.

Dhirendra Kumar
Founder and Chief Executive
Value Research
May 2023

Introduction: Compounding and Inflation

Let's begin with a thought experiment. Say you're earning enough to have some savings, and you are patient enough to wait for your savings to grow. However, you know very little about the way money works, and you don't really have either the time or the inclination to learn all the ins and outs of finance.

Don't worry.

If you pick a set of equity mutual funds and keep investing your savings regularly, given enough time, your net worth will multiply by a huge amount due to the power of compounding. If you pick the right funds, you won't have to spend much time tracking your portfolio. And thanks to digitization, you can invest your savings with a few clicks or swipes and track your investments just as easily.

In the following chapters, we'll explain how mutual funds work and why you should use these instruments.

We'll also explain how you can pick the funds you need and the methods you can use to invest your savings in the most efficient way possible. But before we explain the hows and whys of mutual funds, you need to understand a few basic concepts that every investor must know. Before you decide how to invest, you must understand your own needs, and you must understand two related concepts – inflation and compounding.

If you think you already understand inflation and compounding, you could skip the next few sections and chapters. But a reminder never does any harm, and we'd advise you to read them anyway.

Here's a golden rule: You must invest

This is imperative. Because of inflation, simply saving is not enough. You can't just leave your cash in a savings account or in fixed deposits. Rising prices (aka inflation) will make your money worth less and less as time goes by. On the other hand, a good investment will not just match inflation, but it will also grow your savings at a rate that exceeds it, thus creating wealth for you.

Undoubtedly, investments – especially in mutual funds – can be risky, but if they are done with some care and knowledge, they can reward you handsomely. Conversely, simply putting your money in the bank may seem safe, but it guarantees a loss of purchasing power in the long term. Making regular investments for a long period enables you to exploit the power of compounding to make you rich.

Compounding

Do you understand the concept of compound interest? Many people think they do but few have an innate, deep understanding of just how powerful compounding is. Compound interest is calculated on interest that has already accumulated and is sometimes called 'interest upon interest'.

The longer compounding continues, the more impressive the returns will be. Compounding is the main reason to make long-term investments.

Understand compounding

- Compounding means that the returns on your investments become part of them and start generating returns as well.
- The arithmetic of compounding means that investments generate disproportionately higher amounts after a few years.
- This attribute – the way compounded returns swell in the long-term is what makes long-term investing especially rewarding.

Let's define exactly what compounding means. As per the economics textbook (or on Wikipedia for that matter), the term 'compound interest' is found with the following definition: Compound interest arises when interest is added to the principal, so that, from that moment on, the interest that has been added also earns interest. This addition of interest to the principal is called compounding.

Although this description uses the word 'interest', the general idea applies equally to all forms of returns.

Investors must appreciate that compounding is about the value of time. As your savings start earning returns, and then the returns on those savings start earning returns, and the returns on those returns also start earning returns, the profits start piling up. Translated into human terms, it means that the earlier you invest, the more you earn. Take a look at the graph on the facing page, showing the trajectory of the early investor vs the late investor.

To understand this a bit better, let's start with an example. Two people with similar incomes start investing, and both get the same returns of 9 per cent compounded. The difference is that one started investing at the age of 25, while the other started at 35. By the time they are each 60 years old, one has been invested for 35 years, while the other has been invested for 25 years. The early investor has seen his initial investment of ₹100 grow to ₹2,041, while the later investor had seen his investment grow to ₹862.

Long-term compounding effects

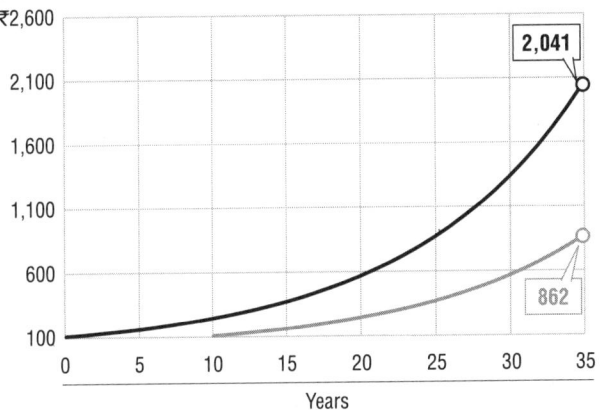

Same principal (₹100). Same interest rate (9%).
Ten extra years for the early investor. More than 2X returns.

Source: Value Research

And so, the important lesson is: **start investing early!**

Inflation also compounds but it compounds 'in reverse', as it were.

Inflation destroys the purchasing power of your savings. Or, if you prefer to think of it another way, as things become more expensive, and the expense compounds, the added cost also becomes more expensive.

If you don't spend 10 per cent of your income every month and simply keep the cash in a box, then you are saving – no question about that – but this won't get you very far. The simple truth is that money doesn't retain value. Prices rise, and what you could buy for ₹100 in 2022 will probably cost ₹108 in 2023.

Historically, inflation in India has always been much higher than in developed countries. Over the last 60 years, inflation has been high in India, and the compounded rate of inflation over this very long period is around 7.5 per cent. This means something worth ₹100 in 2022 becomes worth ₹107.5 in 2023. Inflation compounds, and the inflation of a single year feeds into the next year, and so on. Assuming the inflation rate in 2023 is 7.5 per cent, that means what cost ₹100 in 2022, will cost ₹115.6 in 2024.

If you bought something for ₹1,000 in 1960, you would need to spend over ₹82,000 in 2023 for the same thing. If you bought something for ₹1,000 in 1983, you would need over ₹17,150 to buy the same thing in 2023.

You might think these examples are repetitive but read through them carefully. If you can, pull out a spreadsheet and set yourself some problems that involve compounding. You really need to internalize compounding and understand how it works, in the same automatic way that you understand 2x2=4.

Compounding and its evil twin, inflation, are the two core concepts in investing. To really understand where you

Introduction: Compounding and Inflation

are in terms of financial stability and your future prospects, you need to be comfortable with both.

For example, let's say, you're earning ₹50,000 a month and saving ₹10,000 of that. Are you doing well? That really depends on the following calculation.

- To correctly judge how much you are really saving, you must take inflation into account. For example, if inflation is running at 8 per cent and your money is in a deposit that earns 9 per cent, then you are really earning only 1 per cent.
- Since inflation compounds (like compound interest), the long-term effect is very large though it's uneven. The same cake of soap which cost ₹5 in 2013 now costs ₹40. Your school where you paid a monthly tuition fee of ₹200 now charges ₹3,750 per month. A haircut which used to cost ₹50 ten years ago, now costs ₹500. Petrol which used to cost ₹30 per litre in 2003 costs ₹100.

What compound interest gives, inflation takes away. Put it another way, inflation is effectively like 'decompound interest'.

Since each year's inflation occurs on top of the previous year's inflation, it means that the effect is just like that of compound interest. Consider the following situations.

- You put ₹1 lakh in a deposit which earns 8 per cent a

year (banks pay compound interest). But inflation also rises to 8 per cent. At this point, your savings are just about keeping pace with inflation.

- Now, suppose inflation exceeds the interest you are earning. What if this goes on for a very long time? Suppose your return is 8 per cent, but inflation stays at 10 per cent and 20 years go by? Your ₹1 lakh becomes ₹4.66 lakh, but things that used to cost ₹1 lakh when you made the investment, 20 years ago, now cost ₹6.72 lakh. The purchasing power of ₹1 lakh has eroded to just ₹69,000. Your investment has made you poorer!

Always account for inflation

One of the most common problems investors have is an inability to account for inflation. People tend to think in nominal terms and the future impact of inflation is awfully hard to internalize. You must always adjust returns for inflation. If you think you'll need ₹1 crore to maintain your desired lifestyle 20 years from now, then you'll actually need to have about ₹4 crore. If you work backwards from that target, you'll need to save about ₹68,000 a month if the returns are 8 per cent. There's no escape from the math. So, over long periods, you need to make investments that are adjusted for inflation.

Introduction: Compounding and Inflation

Every investor knows that equity is risky. But inflation is even riskier.

To match inflation, and to get real returns which top it, you must latch on to something that goes up with inflation anyway. This is not so difficult to do. The value of goods, services and assets in the economy is inherently linked to inflation. And so, while equity may be risky, equity and equity-linked investments are the only game in town to protect yourself reliably from inflation.

The rule of 72

Here's a little tip: google 'rule of 72', a formula that makes rough mental calculations of compounding and inflation easier. Sure, you can punch numbers into a calculator or a spreadsheet for exact values, but if you're mentally geared to doing the approximations, you'll get better at internalizing the impact.

The rule of 72 tells you how long it takes a given sum to double at a given rate of return. Alternatively (but it's the same calculation, really), it tells you what rate of return you're receiving if a sum doubles in a given number of years.

For example: Let's say, an investment offers a return of 8 per cent compounded. Then, your money will double in nine years (divide 72 by 8). Or, let's say some investment promises to double your money in five years. Then you're receiving roughly 14.5 per cent return compounded (divide 72 by 5).

In these examples above, you are looking at doubling your money. Now let's say you assume the rate of inflation will remain at 7.5 per cent. Now you can estimate that the purchasing power of your money will fall by roughly 50 per cent in a little under 10 years (divide 72 by 7.5.) Looking 20 years down the line, your money will buy roughly 25 per cent of what it buys today. Remember the calculation above where we said the value of ₹1 crore today will be the same as the value of ₹4 crore, 20 years later? This is the calculation.

To stay ahead of inflation, you must find ways to compound your savings at a faster rate. So, what sort of assets can you invest your savings in?

Anything into which we can put in money and have it grow can be called an investment. Most of us are familiar with the types of things, or assets as they are called, that we can invest in. These could be property, gold, bank deposits, shares in companies, as well as various other types of financial instruments. You might even buy commodities like sugar, or precious stones, or even art.

Be ambitious in your investment goals

Simply matching inflation should not be the goal. Anyone who takes the trouble to learn some of the basics of investing and applies them sensibly should be able to earn more than enough to beat inflation. And if you let your investments accumulate, they can grow over time to create serious wealth.

Take the example on page 6 where we explained that the purchasing power of ₹1,000 in 1983 was equivalent to the purchasing power of ₹17,150 now.

Now let's suppose that same ₹1,000 had been invested in 1983 in the shares of the 30 largest listed companies in India. Its value would have grown at the same rate as the Sensex (which tracks the shares of 30 of the largest listed companies). That ₹1,000 would today (May 2023) have grown to ₹6,17,490 – over ₹6 lakh! This is far, far ahead of inflation since ₹6 lakh can buy you a lot more today than ₹1,000 could have ever bought in 1983.

Investing over long periods of time will not just protect you from inflation – it can make you seriously rich. That's the power of compounding.

Be realistic in your investment goals

Investing can be risky just as it can be rewarding. Newcomers who start investing with over-optimistic expectations, and without enough knowledge or caution, can lose an awful amount of money very quickly. Companies can go bankrupt, or an investor might use a high-risk instrument. You need to be realistic in setting targets and need to minimize risks even while investing. This book will help you avoid most of these pitfalls.

Towards this aim, mutual funds present the safest route to growing your savings and turning them into a fortune. Our goal is to explain the potential returns and the risks and to suggest the options that will help you to invest safely and confidently.

Summary

- Start investing early. Compounding will make you rich.
- If you don't invest, inflation will make you poorer.
- Be ambitious but realistic in your investing goals.

1

Your Needs

What do you need from your investments?

Before you pick your investments, you need to understand your needs and you need to classify the need to select the right investments. For example, you could be saving for emergency medical funds, which could be required at a moment's notice, or you could be saving for your retirement which could be a few decades away, or anything in between.

There is a huge variety of possibilities available when we want to invest and it isn't possible to make sensible choices without thinking about what you need. For example, let's say you need a certain sum, six months later, to send your child to college abroad. There's no point investing in a fixed deposit, which has a one-year tenure.

This is an absurd example of course, but investors frequently do make mistakes of this nature when they invest without working out their own specific needs before selecting an investment from that vast menu of options. They mess up in terms of assessing the time period, as well as in judging how much cash they will need, and also in figuring out how much risk they can afford to take.

You need to know what sort of cash you might need in the short-term to medium-term (less than five years would be our definition of 'short- to medium-term'). And, you also need to grow your investments in the long-term to beat the looming threat of inflation.

At Value Research, we have created a useful framework for classifying these needs. We divide investment needs into four levels: basic contingency funds, term insurance funds, savings for short-term goals and savings for long-term goals. Think of this as a four-storey house. You can't build the first floor without first ensuring that the ground floor is structurally sound.

Similarly, you must meet the needs outlined at each level before going on to the next one. Those who know a bit about psychology may recognize this system as one that is based on the 'Hierarchy of Needs', a concept proposed by the psychologist Abraham Maslow.

So here's Value Research's **hierarchy of investing needs**:

- **Level 1: Basic contingency funds**
  This is money you may need to handle a personal emergency. It should be available instantly, partly as physical cash and partly as funds that can be accessed immediately from a bank. (Despite technology and India's vow to go cashless, there are times and situations when UPI doesn't work and places where net banking isn't available and credit cards are not accepted.)

- **Level 2: Term insurance**
  Work out what your dependents would need to finance short-term life goals and medium-term life goals if you were to suddenly and unexpectedly die, or be struck down by a debilitating injury or disease. This should be a realistic amount. Take out term insurance to cover this. (Term insurance is a no-frills policy that gives your nominee the desired cover if you pass away. If you don't die before the policy expires, you don't get your money back. This is the cheapest and best form of insurance. We'll explain why in a later chapter.)

- **Level 3: Savings for foreseeable short-term goals**
  This is money that you need for expenses that will crop up within the next two to three years. A large part of this should be in minimal-risk deposit-type savings instruments. For example, if you have a child who is

due to enter college or is about to get married, the money should be reliably there on tap.

- **Level 4: Investments for long-term foreseeable goals**
This is similar to Level 3 but the targets are more than three to five years away. Money allocated to this level should be invested in equity and equity-backed investments like equity mutual funds.

One could slice and dice and think of many other levels beyond these and, really, the details matter much less than the concept of defining the basic needs. Depending on one's life circumstances, any of the levels may have to be modified for individual needs.

Important: Remember this framework does not indicate how much you need to allocate to each level. The point is to fulfil the lower levels before you go to the higher levels.

If you have no dependents, you may not need term insurance. If you don't have a child to put through college, your need for Level 3 needs may be less. On the other hand, if you're in a risky profession, you may need a larger Level 1 component.

The point is, if you haven't put emergency cash in a savings account, don't buy term insurance. If you don't have term insurance, don't start putting away money for your daughter's college education, and so on.

In this book, we'll mostly deal with the specific investments needed for fulfilling Level 3 and Level 4, but you can't get there without first taking care of Level 1 and Level 2.

Summary

First steps:

- Work out your personal hierarchy of needs.
- Make sure you fulfil every level before you address the next one.

2

Risk, Reward and Liquidity

Investments can be classified in many ways. For instance, you can think of an investment in terms of how your money is used: do you own part of a business (equity) or are you lending money to someone (debt)? You can also think of investments in terms of risk, returns and liquidity. You need to use a combination of such classifications to identify investments suitable to fulfil your specific needs.

Comparing types of investments

Unless you're running your own business, there are just three basic ways that an investment can make money. One, by lending money to someone who pays interest on it, be it a business or the government. Two, by becoming a part owner of a business, as in by owning shares. And three, by buying something that becomes more valuable, like gold or real estate.

Every sort of investment, no matter how different it may look on the surface, boils down to just these three components and, sometimes, to a combination of these components. There are investments where a loan can be converted into shares in a business, for instance, or you can buy land and earn an income from it and hope the value of the land appreciates as well.

The first step of understanding an investment is to break it down and think of the investment in these terms: is it a share of a business, or a loan of some description or something that might gain in value?

Here are the basic differences between the three types of investments:

- When you own shares (or equity, as it is called) in a business, you can make big profits if the business does well or you can make losses if it does badly. The risks are high, and the potential reward (or 'return' as we would more commonly describe it) is also high. Some businesses do pay dividends out of the profits they make – this will give you an income as well as the potential for profits; other businesses plough profits straight back into the business so that it may grow faster. In the first case, you may get an income, and in the second, you may get faster growth.
- When you lend to a business (by making a bank deposit, for example, or by subscribing to a corporate debenture, or a government bond), your gains are

limited to the interest income the business agrees to pay. No matter how successful that business may become, you are not going to get more than that. So the rewards are predictable, and there's a ceiling to the return. But the business has a legal obligation to pay you. Therefore, unless it goes bankrupt or defrauds you, you get that guaranteed sum.

- In the third kind of investment, the risks and returns are the easiest to intuitively understand. You buy something, such as a house, or some gold or silver. If the price of that goes up at a rate that outruns inflation, that's great. And if it goes down or doesn't keep pace with inflation, you lose money. Of course, if you can earn an income as well (such as rental income from a property), that's well and good.

The jargon

In investing jargon, type 1 (lending) is called debt investing, or **fixed-income investing**.

Type 2 (owning) is called **equity investing**, with stock or shares being synonyms for equity.

These are different 'asset types'. Almost everything that you invest in can be classified as one of these asset types. For example, bank deposits or company deposits are debt, while buying shares or investing in equity mutual funds is equity.

Risk, returns and liquidity

While investments differ from each other in multiple ways, there are three basic characteristics that strongly define any investment. These are **risk**, **returns** and **liquidity**.

Here's what they mean:

Risk: The likelihood of an investment not fetching the return you expect

Returns: How much return does an investment fetch? Remember, it should be inflation-adjusted.

Liquidity: How quickly can you cash out the asset (whether at profit or loss) at any given time?

Of course, there are nuances to each of these factors. **Risk** can be defined as the likelihood of loss of capital, as well as the likelihood of not getting the expected return.

Generally speaking, debt has lower risks and equity has higher risks. However, there are many variations. For example, a debt investment in a business that could go bankrupt is obviously risky, and there are many different levels of risk in equity.

For example, you could invest in a business such as Paytm, which is high-risk because it is trying to create entirely new markets by using digital data. Or, you might invest in a predictable business like National Thermal Power Corporation Limited (NTPC) which generates and sells electricity. If Paytm is successful, it could give you terrific returns and multiply your money, whereas NTPC will just give steady returns. On the other hand, Paytm has a high risk of failure and bankruptcy, while NTPC is extremely unlikely to ever fail.

The attached chart indicates how much more risky and how much more potentially rewarding Paytm could be, compared to NTPC.

Stability vs volatility

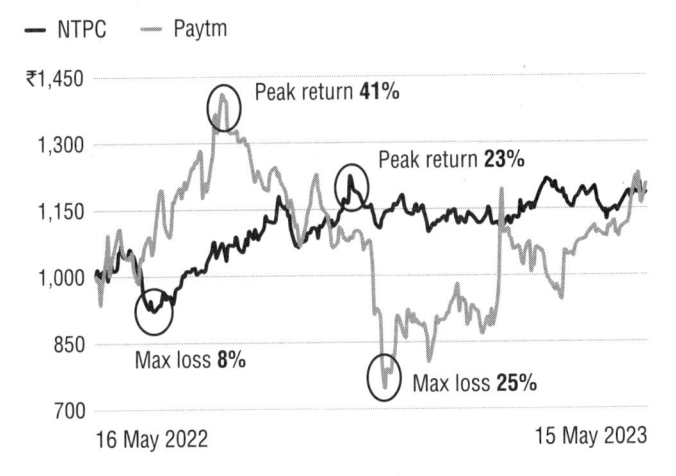

— NTPC   — Paytm

Peak return **41%**
Peak return **23%**
Max loss **8%**
Max loss **25%**

16 May 2022 — 15 May 2023

Investment of ₹1,000 on 16 May 2022

In the last year, NTPC and Paytm (One97 Comm) have gained 18.7% and 20.65%, respectively. But Paytm has been much more volatile, with maximum drop of 25% and a peak return of 41%, while NTPC has been relatively stable with maximum gain of 23% and maximum loss of 8%.

Source: Value Research

Returns are the main goal of any investment and they are the flip side of risk.

Usually, higher returns come with higher risk. Again, the defining example of this is the debt-to-equity comparison. Debt investments have less risk and lower returns, while equity can deliver higher returns but with higher risk attached.

Do note that we say equity 'can' have higher returns compared to debt – there are no guarantees. There are huge variations within equity and it's perfectly possible to make an equity investment that carries higher risk while giving poor returns. In fact, that's the toxic combination that careless or overconfident equity investors end up with.

Liquidity, the third part of the investing triad, is not always that important to every investor in every situation. In some investments you can immediately get your money back. For example, if you keep your money in a savings bank account, you can walk into an ATM and immediately withdraw it (subject to some limits). If you go to the bank, you can withdraw all of it immediately.

In some investments, there can be a penalty for liquidity. Take a fixed deposit, for instance, where you either wait for the agreed term or you settle for lower returns if you 'break' the deposit early.

Risk, Reward and Liquidity

Liquidity can get more complex. In equity, liquidity varies from stock to stock. You can sell off the shares of a big company instantly, but for smaller companies (or companies with few outstanding shares – that is, shares that are not owned by the promoters or institutions) it may take time to find a buyer for a large chunk of shares.

Mutual fund liquidity is generally pretty good for most categories of funds – it is almost akin to equity shares for open-ended funds. In general, you can redeem mutual fund units and get your money back within three working days. However, there may be a lock-in period for a new scheme.

A concept somewhat like liquidity is **divisibility**. Some investments, like real estate, may have to be sold in the same quantity as when they were bought. Generally speaking, it's difficult to sell only part of an apartment (though it is possible if you have a large parcel of land). But shares can be sold in smaller chunks. Depending on your needs, divisibility may or may not be important. For example, you may own, say, 1,000 shares in a given company. You can, in theory, sell the equity investment off at 1 share at a time.

Throughout this book, we'll keep harking back to these concepts, especially to risk, reward and liquidity, when we describe and classify possible investments.

Benchmarks

Risk and return need to be compared to a 'risk-free benchmark' of return and inflation to be meaningful.

Where inflation is concerned, we generally look at the prevailing Consumer Price Index (CPI). Data for this is released on a monthly basis. As mentioned earlier in the introduction, India's inflation compounds at around 7.5–8 per cent.

Your individual lifestyle may have a different cost of living. The CPI looks at many goods and services spread across categories like food, transport, clothing, housing, etc., and it assumes the 'average' person spends, say, 45 per cent of their income on food and 25 per cent on housing.

Your personal expenditure patterns may be quite different. You may spend less on food but more on housing, or more on transport, for example. But you can use the monthly CPI data, or the rough yardstick of a long-term rate of 8 per cent inflation, as a benchmark when considering any investment.

For most individuals, it's usual to compare returns from investments to the fixed-deposit rates their bank offers for the same time frame they intend to invest. The interest from a fixed deposit is usually less than inflation but the principal is safe with the bank and hence, it's 'risk free'.

You can also buy government treasuries (through a mutual fund) and those are even safer than bank deposits if held till maturity. The central government borrows money for various tenures via auctions run by the Reserve Bank. So do states and municipalities. The Post Office and the Provident Funds also borrow money on behalf of the central government. Various government-run enterprises and institutions such as the National Highways Authority of India and the Indian Railways (through its subsidiaries) also borrow money. Since these loans are taken with a government guarantee, these may be reckoned very safe.

But of course, no investment is entirely risk-free. Big economic tsunamis can lead to hyperinflation or to currency fluctuations that make an entire nation poorer, or even lead a government to defaulting on its debt, for example. Look at Argentina, for example – banks there are offering 97 per cent interest on fixed deposits (May 2023) because inflation is running at nearly triple digits.

Summary

- Every investment is either equity, debt or value, or a mix of these three categories.
- Work out the expected risk and reward. Compare these to a risk-free benchmark.
- Higher returns generally come with higher risks attached.
- Make sure the risk, reward and liquidity of a specific investment works for you.

3

Asset Allocation

As discussed in the previous chapter, there are just three broad ways in which an investment can make money. One, by lending money to someone who pays interest. Two, by becoming an owner or part-owner of a business, as in by holding shares in it. And three, by buying something that becomes more valuable in future, like gold or real estate.

These are different types of assets with different risks, returns and liquidity. Also within these broad parameters, there are many different types of assets, each with its own risk and return equation.

An investor must assess their own needs and mix and match the combination of assets. This is called **asset allocation.** When the needs change, or when economic circumstances change, or when the ratio changes due to divergent returns, investors need to consider shifting allocations. This is **asset rebalancing.**

Asset allocation and rebalancing help control risks and cope with volatility.

Step one of understanding any potential investment is to think of it in these terms. Figure out if the investment is debt or equity, or if it's a play for long-term gains in value. Then make a guess at the likely risks and returns from holding this asset.

As long as you can take this first step of understanding, you've made a good start in figuring out whether it's the right investment for you.

Here are the basic differences in terms of risks and returns between the three categories:

1. Equity investing

When you own shares in a business, you can either make big profits if the business does well or make losses if the business does badly. The risks are high, and the potential of reward is also high.

While buying shares makes you a part-owner, you may have too small a stake to have a say in how the business is run, though you will be allowed to vote on some decisions as a shareholder.

But the financial rewards (on per-share basis) are the same for every owner. When the business pays out part of its profits as dividend, then as part-owner you get your share. When the business becomes more valuable (the price of its shares increases), your wealth increases.

Also, like any business owner, you can decide to sell off all or some of your shares of ownership, or hold them for future gains. Those future gains could be in the form of dividends, or even further increases in the price of the shares.

Conversely, if the value of the shares goes down, you could lose money. If the business does very badly, you could lose a large chunk of your initial investment. (This initial investment is often called the principal, by the way, and we've used that term quite a few times.)

So equity investments have the following characteristics:

- Large risks, large rewards
- High liquidity
- Potential for income via dividends
- Potential for capital gains if the price of the share increases
- Potential for capital loss if the price falls

2. Debt investing

Lending money to someone has very different characteristics as an investment. Note that unlike in the case of shares, we didn't say 'lending money to a business'. Instead, we said 'lending money to someone'.

That's because you could be lending not just to a business but to a government or some other entity. When we say lending, it includes activities that you may not normally think of as a loan. Lending just means giving someone money and getting interest income in return.

For example, depositing money and getting interest on it is lending. When you make a deposit in a bank (it could be a fixed deposit or just a savings account), you are lending money to the bank. When you make a post office deposit or a Public Provident Fund (PPF) deposit, you are lending to the Government of India.

The scope of gains from a loan is very limited compared to investing in shares. When you lend to a business (by making a bank deposit, for example), your gains are limited to the interest rate that the business has agreed to pay you. No matter how successful that business may become, you are not going to get more than that. Of course, the risks are limited too. In most kinds of deposits, the risk of losing money or not getting your interest is rather limited.

So the rewards are predictable and so are the risks.

3. Value plays

In the third kind of investment, the risks and rewards are the easiest to understand. You buy something. If the price goes up that's great. But if it goes down, you lose money. You may also get an income, such as rental income from a property.

Picking and choosing

In terms of actually choosing an investment, the complexities are of different scales depending on the investment. Equity is vastly more complex compared to the others. There are literally thousands of companies whose shares you could buy from the stock markets, and it's not easy to make the right choices.

Fortunately, there are ways to avoid making choices yourself by using mutual funds. Fund managers – professional investors who study the market intensively – can make the choices for you.

Asset rebalancing

Asset rebalancing must be among the most useful and yet the most ignored of ideas in the world of investing. However, it's actually so easy to implement, especially for mutual fund investors, that it's worthwhile to periodically revisit the concept and see whether it can be applied to your portfolio.

Asset rebalancing is the right response to situations where the prospects of equity are dubious but fixed-income investing looks like a good option or vice versa.

Currently, it's relatively straightforward to earn say, 6 to 8 per cent (nominally, without adjusting for inflation) from a wide variety of fixed-income options, both guaranteed ones and market-linked ones.

Among mutual funds, almost all debt fund categories are returning an average of 6.5 to 8 per cent per annum. So if you're looking at equity, you must have expectations of a higher return since there's a higher risk.

But that's a simplistic view. Rather than checking month to month and tweaking your asset allocation, it's better to do this mechanically in an automated way for the longer-term.

You should decide that a certain percentage of your investments should be in fixed income and the rest in equity. For younger investors, who are many years away from retirement, the fixed income proportion could be low, as low as 10 per cent, or even less. **But it shouldn't be zero.**

For those with a more conservative approach, or older people who are approaching retirement or already retired, the fixed income component should be higher.

However, whatever the initial ratio you set, it will change over time, because fixed income and equity give contrasting returns. There will be periods when equity returns will be low or negative, and periods when equity returns could be very high.

Asset rebalancing means that instead of seeing the equity-vs-fixed question as a black-vs-white binary

choice, you should be seeing it as shades of grey. Every year or so, you should 'rebalance' your portfolio.

What this means is that if the actual balance has veered away from your desired one, you should shift money from one asset category to the other in order to come back to your desired percentage again.

To take a hypothetical example, let's say you decide to keep a ratio of 90:10 with respect to equity and debt. You put 10 per cent of your savings into a fixed income instrument that pays 7 per cent per annum and you put the remaining 90 per cent into an equity fund which returns 25 per cent in that year. At the end of a year, your original equity investment is now worth around 91.3 per cent of your entire portfolio. You may want to book profits on that 'excess 1.3 per cent' and put that into debt to keep the 90:10 allocation ratio. By the way, if you remember about divisibility, this is one of the places where it's useful. You can sell a small proportion of your portfolio to rebalance.

Book profits and rebalance

When equity is growing faster than fixed income – which is what you would expect most of the time – you should periodically sell some equity investments and invest that money in fixed income, so that the balance is restored.

When equity starts lagging, you periodically sell some

of your fixed income assets and move the money into equity.

This beautifully implements the basic idea of booking profits and investing in the beaten-down asset.

Economies operate in cycles and different assets perform well or badly at different points in a cycle. Inevitably, returns revert to a mean – that means that when an asset category is outperforming, you should book some profits, and when an asset is lagging, you should invest more.

Asset rebalancing does this automatically if you are disciplined about it.

Time and taxes

Some readers must have seen the fly in the ointment. Or rather, two flies! One, rebalancing requires some amount of monitoring and work. Two, there are tax implications to booking profits.

Again, this is a situation where mutual funds can be useful in that they help you to seamlessly accomplish the twin tasks of monitoring and rebalancing. There's a category of mutual funds called balanced funds (also called hybrid funds and we'll use the two terms interchangeably) that invest across both fixed income and equity.

So, if you don't want to go through the time and trouble to do all this yourself, you can just invest in a balanced fund and that takes cares of asset allocation without building up tax liability. The fund will ensure that the balancing is done and mutual funds don't pay taxes on their trades.

The tax factor incidentally is a major reason why you don't rebalance too often if you're doing it all yourself. Broadly you pay far lower taxes on profits from equity (called 'capital gains') if you've held the investment for over a year. If, instead, you hold a balanced fund that does the rebalancing for you, you don't pay taxes. If you look at rebalancing yourself, you need to calculate the tax liability and figure out if it's worth doing this.

The secret sauce of balanced funds

Importantly, when the stock market goes down, balanced funds fall less than pure equity funds. Over the last few years, when there've been huge upheavals in the equity markets, the average equity-oriented balanced fund has given better returns than the diversified equity funds.

While balanced funds typically invest more than 65 per cent of their assets in equity for tax reasons, less aggressive rebalancing options are also available. Some balanced funds that offer Monthly Income Plans (we'll explain those later) typically keep the equity proportion at less than 20 per cent or so and these are a very good option for more conservative investors.

Summary

- Decide what your needs are and set your asset allocation accordingly.
- Keep some investments in every category.
- Set a ratio between fixed income and equity that suits you.
- Periodically rebalance to ensure that your overall asset allocation ratio remains close to what you had decided.
- You can use balanced funds to reallocate painlessly without incurring big tax implications.

4

Understanding Your Needs

Unless you think carefully about your needs and understand what investments will fulfil them, it's not possible to choose the right investments. Being clear about your goals and deciding on the appropriate investment objectives is crucial, and many people falter at this stage. The importance of doing this analysis well and how to do it is demonstrated in the following example, which a Value Research analyst encountered while studying real-world investment portfolios.

The investors in question were a retired couple who, despite having a good understanding of investing, were unable to figure out whether they were on the right track. They had investments in a number of funds, which were mostly equity oriented. Using these investments, they had to meet a number of needs including:

- A regular monthly income to meet household expenses
- Emergency funds that could be withdrawn at short notice
- Large family-related expenses coming up in about three years
- Funding their lifestyle in the long run, which means funding monthly expenses far into the future as prices rose and their needs changed

The plan they needed was nothing out of the ordinary, but they were still not confident that their portfolio was the right one for their needs. Even though this couple had chosen good funds, they were having problems understanding whether they were on the right track.

But that wasn't their fault. Understanding how an investment portfolio maps to a set of different needs is a complex task, and it may seem overwhelmingly difficult when you do it for the first time. Also, some needs are often contradictory. For example, short-term income needs demand stability and safety from your investments. But for the long-term nest egg, high returns are more important.

Let's say you're looking at a short list of 10 funds and calculating systematic investment plans (SIPs), dividends and considering withdrawals of varying amounts, working out different performance and quality levels, and balancing different expectations of risk and returns. There are so many possible permutations and possibilities it seems impossible to figure out, even roughly, whether a given portfolio will do the job. All you can do is to look at the overall value of the portfolio and you might get panicky if it begins to decline.

So what then is the solution to this problem? A sophisticated analytical tool? No, it's something that someone in your family probably already practises, or at least used to practise. Indeed, it's something that the elderly couple already knew and were practising. They just hadn't realized that it fit this situation as well!

The solution is bags. Yes, that's right – bags.

Do you have an elderly relative in your family who saves money by putting it in little bags, each bag allocated for a different purpose? Think about it, and you'll know many grandmas and aunts who have run their household finances like this. They typically have little pouches with a drawstring around the top. When their husbands handed over money for household expenses, they put some money in the vegetables pouch, some in the milk pouch, some in the domestic workers' pouch, and the laundry pouch, and so on. There would also be a few bigger pouches meant for long-term expenses, such as family weddings. The money in this pouch would be converted into gold jewellery every few months.

Financially sophisticated readers will call this system primitive and suboptimal, but it has a lot going for it. It is a simple system, easy to implement, easy to understand and above all, it *works*.

Most importantly, it incorporates one of the golden rules of personal investment management – separate portfolios for separate goals.

A portfolio is simply a collection of investments, and your entire set of investments is your complete portfolio. We'd recommend that you think of portfolios like your aunt's little pouches. Funnily enough, the word 'portfolio' originally meant a leather bag designed to carry documents, and so those little pouches are literally like mini-portfolios.

Separating your money and allocating it into different portfolios helps you to tailor each portfolio to perform a specific task. Money for some expenses should be kept in the bank, while some other cash can be parked in mutual funds, or land, or something else. You can bet that your aunt would not have managed her household in such an organized manner if she had kept all her money in one big bag.

If you can use that principle and put your finances into several different portfolios, you will be able to manage your investments better. Instead of physical bags, you can use spreadsheets or simple handwritten notes – or just keep them separate in your head, for that matter. Some people even set up separate bank accounts to account for different portfolios though that may seem like an extreme solution since keeping the tax paperwork and passwords straight for multiple bank accounts can be quite a chore.

Summary

- Investing without understanding one's exact needs is inefficient.
- Once you've worked out what you want, split your savings and investments into different mini-portfolios.

5

What Are Mutual Funds?

Many years ago, my father and his brothers were all looking to buy or construct houses. They consulted with one of their cousins, an architect, who advised them to pool their budgets and buy a plot where they could construct separate houses. This enabled them all to get a much better deal than they would have separately

Mutual funds do something similar. These investment vehicles pool the savings of a large number of investors and manage that money as a single corpus. These are run by professionals – fund managers who understand how to invest and do it full-time. The individual investors in a mutual fund need not worry about choosing stocks, bonds or commodities to invest in; the fund managers do this for them.

Mutual funds are floated and run by companies known as asset management companies (AMCs). Each AMC may operate a number of funds suited to different types of investment needs. As of June 2023, there are 40 AMCs in India running over 1,500 mutual funds between them. Together, they manage over ₹40 lakh crores (or ₹40 trillion) in assets spread across 146 million **folios** (a folio is the mutual fund equivalent of a bank account – every investor has a folio where her mutual funds are listed).

For the individual investor who doesn't have much time to study and research investments themselves, mutual funds are by far the best option for reaping the benefits of different types of investments with a minimum of effort and low entry points. Most funds allow minimum subscriptions as low as ₹500 or ₹1,000. Also, unlike many other types of assets, mutual fund investments are highly 'liquid', meaning that an investor can withdraw from a fund within a day.

Multiple types of mutual funds

There are many, many types of mutual funds with a wide range of risk levels, profit potential and, of course, different qualities of management. They invest in everything from the stocks of publicly listed companies to corporate bonds, government debt and even overseas assets.

As you would expect, mutual funds that invest in equity offer the highest potential returns but with the

What Are Mutual Funds?

highest possible risk. At the other extreme of the return range are the funds that invest in short-term bonds and deposits, which offer returns that are in the same rough range as bank fixed deposits, but with a high degree of safety.

The table below lists the sort of returns you can expect over time from different assets. We've listed different assets, mentioned the category or type, mentioned the sort of return an investor may typically expect and assessed the level of risk. Risk in this case means the chance of loss of principal. Finally, we've compared these assets to inflation.

Beating inflation

Asset	Category	Compounded return (%) 10 years	Risk	Does it beat inflation at 8.5%?
Small-cap equity fund*	Equity fund	20.63	Very high	Yes
Aggressive hybrid fund*	65% equity	13.08	Medium	Yes
Large-cap equity fund*	Equity fund	12.98	High	Yes
Sensex	Equity index	12.39	High	Yes
Conservative hybrid fund*	20% equity	8.28	Low	Maybe
Long-duration debt fund*	Debt fund	6.91	Low	No
Bank fixed deposit	Debt	6.50	Very low	No

*Category average as on 6 June 2023.

If you want to beat inflation in the long term, you need to accept some risk. These are typical risk return profiles of some asset classes.

Source: Value Research

The mutual fund industry is regulated by the Securities and Exchange Board of India (SEBI), which also regulates the stock market and the bond market and sets norms for listed companies and traders. SEBI has strict guidelines for AMCs. For example, funds have to declare the categories of assets they will invest in and the ratio of such assets in their portfolios; the funds have ceilings on expenses; the funds must declare portfolios regularly, and declare the value of portfolios on a daily basis. Moreover, employees are forbidden to indulge in crimes like front-running (buying a stock on their individual account just before the fund buys the stock) or insider trading (using price-sensitive information that is not public to trade).

Funds issue **units** to subscribers. Units are like shares – just like any investment in a company is divided into shares, the investment in a fund is divided into units. Also, like companies, funds have initial offers (**New Fund Offers** or **NFO** in the jargon) when they launch, when you can buy units at the face-value price (usually ₹10 per unit). So, if you subscribe to a new fund offering for ₹1,000, you will receive 100 units.

Every fund has a **mandate**. At the time it is launched, it declares what it will invest in, and it offers a **benchmark** for the comparison of returns. It also declares its **expense ratio (**which must be within the limits set by the SEBI), which is the percentage of cash it uses for expenses.

AMCs keep launching new schemes and funds. A fund can have several schemes, which allow investors to put their money in and take it out in different ways at their convenience. For example, some funds offer monthly or quarterly income options, meaning that a percentage of the returns earned is distributed (like companies distribute dividends) to investors. Others just keep ploughing the returns back into buying more assets.

Some funds are **open-ended**. This means you can subscribe any time after the launch of the fund and withdraw your money at any time. Other schemes are **closed-ended,** meaning that the fund will not issue new units after an initial subscription.

Every fund must declare a **net asset value** or **NAV** on a daily basis as well as declare the assets in their portfolio every quarter. The assets held by the mutual funds are divided by the total number of units issued. For example, let's say a fund has raised ₹10,000 by selling 1,000 units. It has then invested that money and received a 10 per cent return (net of expenses). So it now has ₹11,000 in assets. This means each unit now has a Net Asset Value of ₹11. The NAV is a key number for investors to track. If you wish to redeem your units, your fund will buy them from you at the NAV at the end of the working day when you make your redemption request.

Apart from a wide variation in the investment focus, there is also a wide diversity in the quality of funds. This means not all funds are able to deliver what they promise, and investors also have to keep an eye on individual funds' track record, their fund managers and fund companies.

Value research can help you do this. We'll explain how later in the book.

The advantages of buying mutual funds

There are a number of advantages to investing in mutual funds, including those listed below.

Instant and easy diversification: One of the basics of safe investing is to spread your money across different investments. Don't put all your eggs in the same basket.

Mutual funds are an easy way to ensure portfolio diversification. Each mutual fund spreads money across a large number of investments.

Professional research and investment management: Investing is a lot of work. There are literally hundreds of companies to track, and their prospects could change without warning. While you could do it yourself, you may not have the time. or the inclination or the skills. Mutual funds employ professional, full-time investment managers and research staff. Their cost and efforts gets shared 'mutually' among all the investors of a fund and is reflected in the expense ratio.

Variety: There are mutual funds for every sort of return-and-risk combination and suitable for every kind of time horizon. No matter what kind of investment you want, there's likely to be a fund or, more likely, many funds that suit you.

Convenience: You can easily make investments as well as withdraw them in any amount that you need. Investments can be made either by filling up a simple form or online with direct debits from your bank account. Similarly, redemptions can be made directly into your bank account and take no more than three days. If you try to directly diversify across a variety of industries and assets, you will need huge sums. However, a mutual fund can help you diversify across dozens of companies for as little as a thousand rupees. What's more, you can invest more (or redeem your money) in small batches.

Tax efficiency: When you directly buy or sell any investments, you must pay tax on the profits you make. However, this is not applicable when the transactions are done by a mutual fund on your behalf. The fund manager can buy and sell stocks as needed, and you pay tax only as and when you redeem your investments from the fund.

Transparent, well-regulated industry: Mutual funds are obligated by law to release comprehensive data about their operations and investments. Almost all funds release NAV status daily, and most actually release their complete portfolio every month (though they are only obliged to do so every quarter). SEBI regulates the mutual fund industry very stringently and is constantly refining the rules to help protect investors better.

Providing access to inaccessible assets: There are many investments you can make only through a fund. For example, individuals cannot buy government bonds easily, but they can buy funds that invest in such bonds. Individuals can buy government bonds from the 'RBI Retail Direct' platform but the process can be very challenging to navigate for someone who is not tech savvy. Hence, better to buy funds that invest in such bonds

It is also complex and difficult to open an overseas brokerage account and buy shares of companies listed in different countries abroad. However, you can do so easily by investing in an international fund.

Some other characteristics of mutual funds which you need to bear in mind:

1. Capital protection

Mutual funds do not offer capital protection in a legally enforceable way. All mutual funds invest in market-linked investments and losses are always possible, even in debt funds. However, AMCs are also allowed to run what are called capital protection-oriented funds, which invest in a high proportion of safe fixed-income securities and a small proportion of equities. Investors who stay invested for the long-term are highly unlikely to suffer any loss of capital.

2. Inflation protection

Mutual funds do not offer any kind of a contractual or formal inflation protection. However, when you invest in well-chosen equity funds for a period of several years or more, your chances of beating inflation are much better than with any other type of investment.

3. Guarantees

There are no guarantees in mutual fund investments as you would know if you've watched the 'Mutual Funds Sahi Hai' campaigns. However, referring to the risk-return table given on page 47, you will realize that different funds carry different levels of risk. You can always find a fund that suits your needs, without taking on excessive risk.

4. Liquidity

As per SEBI's rules, all mutual funds must offer liquidity. However, the liquidity can be of different natures, depending on whether a fund is open-ended or close-ended.

Open-ended funds are perpetual funds that are always available for investment or redemption with the AMC, but remember that many funds have a six-month lock-in period at the time of the issue. For open-ended funds, the AMC will redeem the money at the NAV-based selling price of the day the redemption request is made. You'll get your money within three working days at most.

Closed-ended funds are launched for a fixed period (generally three to ten years), and you can invest in them only during the initial offer. For these funds, the AMCs usually have the fund listed on a stock exchange so that you can sell your units like a stock through a stockbroker. However, redeeming units like this is usually not a great option because the stock-exchange price of a unit is generally at a big discount from the NAV.

In practice, you should buy into a closed-ended fund only if you're prepared to be locked in for the full duration.

Also, it is not possible to take them in an **SIP**. You must make an initial large lump sum investment, rather than putting in small sums every month as you can in an open-ended fund.

Tax-saving funds save you tax as per Section 80C of the Income Tax Act, but you cannot redeem them during the three-year lock-in period as per the income tax rules.

5. Credit rating

There is no mandatory credit rating for mutual funds. Fixed-income funds may publicize a rating they receive from a rating agency, but this has no legal standing. It is little more than a marketing device.

6. Value Research ratings

While there's no formal legal rating system for funds, if you need a simple, easy-to-understand rating system that tells you how good or bad a fund is, **Value Research's Fund Rating System** has been helping investors find this out for over 25 years.

At Value Research, we track public data and evaluate funds on a range of parameters to not only evaluate the long-term returns generated but also its riskiness. To assess risk, we compare the returns to a 'risk-free asset', such as the interest paid by the State Bank of India on fixed deposits. The funds are then graded on five levels ranging from 1 Star to 5 Star according to our system.

This is a relative rating calculated in comparison to other funds of the same type. Our methodology is transparent and described in detail on our website, and we update our ratings continuously. There is no subjectivity – we analyse performance data and compare funds. In addition to the millions of regular visitors on our website, the mutual fund industry also uses our ratings extensively.

7. Load

The load is a small percentage of your invested funds that can be deducted by the AMC at the time of redemption. Load percentages are generally low, and the actual percentage (and whether a load is charged at all) depends on the type of fund and the period for which the investment has been held. Typically, there could be a load of 1 per cent if you redeem within a year of investment and no load after that.

8. Taxation

There is a specific fund known as an equity-linked savings scheme (ELSS) fund, which is a permissible investment under Section 80C of the Income Tax Act. ELSS funds have a lock-in of three years, and apart from these, other types of mutual funds have tax liabilities depending on the type of assets they invest in. The most important thing to understand is that when you redeem an equity fund you have held for more 12 months, then the gains are taxed at a rate of 10 per cent whereas the same are taxed at 15 per cent if held for a shorter period. For debt, overseas assets and hybrid funds (funds which invest in more than one type of asset), any profits are simply added to your taxable income and taxed at the applicable rate.

These are the rules at the time of writing (May 2023), but the tax treatment of assets can change at any time, and you should always check the relevant tax rules in case there's a change or update.

Summary

- Mutual funds are an easy way for investors to gain the benefits of investing without having to do much research or analysis.
- Mutual funds offer diversification, convenience, tax efficiency and several other benefits.
- There are mutual funds available to suit a wide variety of investing needs.

6

Systematic Investment

Apart from the straightforward investment and redemption in mutual funds, there are a few special 'systematic' ways of investing and redeeming your money in these instruments, which can be enormously useful. They ensure you invest in more disciplined ways and help enhance returns.

To understand why systematic investment is better, **look at the chart below. That's the Nifty Index over the last 10 years (since January 2013, about 10 years and 5 months**; see figure on the next page).

The Nifty Index tracks the averaged returns of the 50 largest listed companies, and it's a good reflection of how the stock market behaves. In this chart, we've given the monthly high–low and closing values (the last reading of the month).

Over that decade, the index has gained 11.4 per cent compounded. But it's not a straight-line progression, as

Equity volatility: Nifty 2013–2023

— Closing price — High — Low

[Chart: Monthly Nifty Data from January 2013 to May 2023, ranging from about 5,000 to 20,000]

Holding for the long term helps to smooth out volatility.
Compounded return: 11.4%; Biggest monthly loss: 23.25%;
Biggest gain: 14.72%; Average monthly move: +1.028%

Source: www.nseindia.com

---

one glance should make clear. **There are periods when the stock market has seen steep drops and also periods of steep climbs. There are periods when the index has lost up to 23 per cent in a month, and also periods when it has gained over 10 per cent in a month.**

We put this chart up to illustrate that stock prices fluctuate a lot, even though they gain a lot in the long run. The Nifty beat inflation comfortably but to reliably profit from this, you had to average your cost price and hold for the long-term, ignoring short-term fluctuations.

Many equity funds will give returns that are similar to the Nifty, both in terms of value as well as in terms of volatility. And knowing about this volatility helps us to understand why SIPs are a good method of investment.

If you make large lump sum investments into equity funds regularly, you could get lucky or unlucky. If you invest at a time when the stock market was down, your returns would be large because your costs are low. However, if you make a large single-payment investment when the market was hitting a peak, you would get poor returns because your costs are high.

A systematic investor avoids this problem by investing equal sums (or roughly equal sums) at regular intervals. That way, their cost price is averaged down and their long-term returns are higher. Also, in practical terms, most of us don't earn in lump sums; we tend to earn relatively smaller sums every month or quarter. This means that it's easier for us to invest systematically every month and because we're putting that money aside, it's good discipline.

Systematic investment, systematic withdrawal and systematic transfer plans

1. **Systematic investment plans (SIPs):** An SIP is a regular investment of a fixed amount that occurs at a fixed frequency, which is generally monthly. SIPs

neatly solve the two major problems that prevent investors from getting decent returns from mutual funds. First, since SIPs mean investing a fixed sum regardless of the NAV or the market level, investors automatically buy more units when the price (NAV) is low. This results in a lower average price, which translates to higher long-term returns, and this avoids the possibility that you'll get saddled with a high NAV as might happen with a single lump sump investment. Thus, an SIP is a good way to invest at an average price over a period.

Second, an SIP is also a great psychological aid to investing. Left to themselves, investors inevitably try to time the market. When the market falls, they assume it will fall even more and they sell their holdings. When it rises, they invest more because they assume it will rise some more. This is exactly the opposite of what a long-term investor should do. An SIP puts an end to this cycle by automating the process of investing regularly. It also eliminates the mental stress of deciding when to invest and thus, leads to better returns.

It always makes sense to use an SIP, and every fund house allows you to set up SIPs. The process isn't difficult and won't take you more than a few minutes online. Once it's done, you can pretty much forget about it. SIPs are a big reason why investors should, in general, prefer open-ended funds since it is impossible to do an SIP into a closed-ended fund – that can only be done with a one-time lump sum investment.

2. **Systematic withdrawal plans (SWPs)**: These plans involve regular redemption from a fund. There are several variations possible in this instrument. Investors can either redeem a fixed amount, or a fixed number of units, or book profits for returns above a certain base level. Among other things, SWPs are a convenient way to reap a regular income from a fund investment. If you have a recurring payment, such as an EMI for a car or a house, an SWP can be useful. It ensures that you will never miss a payment date. These plans are also commonly used by elderly people who have invested consistently and now wish to slowly liquidate their long-term investments to sustain their lifestyles.

    Finally, SWPs are also useful in the context of the next instrument we will discuss – the systematic transfer plan.

3. **Systematic transfer plans (STPs)**: An STP is a regular transfer from one fund to another. It's like an SIP, but the source of the money for investment is an SWP from another fund. The most frequent use of an

STP occurs when you have a lump sum – for example, you've inherited some money or you've received a bonus at work – to invest in an equity fund.

As we've explained above, it is always better to invest gradually via a SIP rather than investing a large sum all at once. In such cases, you can put the lump sum in a debt fund so that it earns some returns and give instructions to transfer a fixed amount into a chosen equity fund (or basket of equity funds) every month. This is called an STP.

Summary

- Regular investing on a schedule offers better returns and several other advantages.
- Funds offer many different ways to manage systematic, scheduled investing.

7

Portfolios and How to Build Them

To understand how to build a portfolio, you first need to understand what the term means and what it implies. By definition, the original meaning of the word, a portfolio is a leather bag, a type of briefcase, designed to carry documents. It became associated with investing because in the early twentieth century, stockbrokers would keep each client's share certificates in a separate portfolio. Thus, the word gradually came to mean any collection of documents. Over the years, however, the meaning evolved to specifically mean the investments held by an investor. But at Value Research, we don't think it makes sense to use the word to simply refer to a collection of all of someone's investments.

A portfolio is much more than a collection of assets. As we've mentioned before, the best way for individuals to plan their investments is to have a separate portfolio set up for each financial goal. As you'll learn, diverse mixes of assets lead to different risk levels and gain expectations. Most people find it difficult to match these risks and rewards to what they want or need. If you're asked what the risk level of your investment is, you'll probably give some sort of answer but the chances are that it will just be a gut feel.

However, if you have specific financial targets in mind and are thinking of the money needed to fulfil them, you will be able answer questions about risk and returns much more precisely. For example, let's say you'll need money for higher education for your daughter in three years. Or you'd like to buy a house at least 10 years before retirement. You'd like to go on a vacation to Europe in 2025. You'd like ₹2 lakh to always be available for emergencies.

Each of these goals is very precise. The risk you can take as well as the money you require can be quantified precisely, and it is relatively easy to decide what kind of investments you should make to fulfil each of these objectives. Thus, rather than thinking of your portfolio as a whole, think instead of the many portfolios you must have to achieve each of your financial goals. Only then can you fine-tune each portfolio's level of conservativeness or aggressiveness to the right level of risk and return.

Another important thing to remember is that a portfolio is not simply a collection of assets. It consists of different parts that must fit together in specific ways and complement each other. You could have three funds that provide the prospect of high gains and two funds for stability. In hindsight, it may appear that you could have stuck with one set or the other. But if you're a sensible investor, both types would have played a role.

In the following sections, we'll learn the basics of constructing a portfolio as well as take a look at some model portfolios. These have been designed to fulfil specific goals, and constructed with a time frame in mind

It's best to divide one's investments into separate portfolios, each constructed with a specific purpose. Value Research has a tool that could help you do this. We'll describe this later on.

When you're constructing a portfolio you need to consider the following things:
- The time frame over which a portfolio should reach its goal is the most important factor determining the investments that should be made.
- For long-term portfolios, equity-based mutual funds are generally an excellent choice.

How to build a portfolio

As we saw in the last section, the first step towards building a portfolio is to have a clear goal for it. In

Value Research's way of thinking, short-term goals are fundamentally different from long-term ones, and these are best fulfilled using fixed-income investments because they are safer and more stable in terms of returns. For example, this asset could be a bank fixed deposit or debt funds. If you are saving gradually towards a goal, the post office recurring deposit is an excellent tool. It currently yields a return of 6.2 per cent per annum.

However, long-term financial goals are best fulfilled using a portfolio comprising equity mutual funds. Equity is the only type of asset that can ensure that your money grows faster than inflation and does not actually lose value in the long term. However, equity mutual funds can be volatile and thus, they are only suitable for long-term investments. In the short term, the ups and downs of stock markets could well lead to temporary losses. As a result, we do not recommend investing in equity mutual funds for these situations. If your financial goal needs to be accomplished in less than about three to five years, equity may be risky.

In the following sections, we'll explain some of the basics of designing a portfolio to fit a particular financial goal. The first step is to see how much you need to invest to reach your objective.

The table below shows how much you need to invest every month to accumulate ₹10 lakh in a specific period.

Let's say you wish to have ₹10 lakh in three years (36 months).

The first column assumes you can invest ₹25,000 per month. Given that as your baseline, where should you invest to get close to ₹10 lakh in 36 months? And what sort of risks are you incurring?

To help you see the difference between different kinds of investments, we have shown the typical returns you can expect from a post office recurring deposit (6.2 per cent compounded), a typical balanced fund (9.5 per cent compounded) and an index equity fund (12.5 per cent compounded) over a period of three years.

Target: ₹10 lakh in three years

Monthly investment (₹)	Type	Expected return (%)	Three-year total invested (₹)	End value (₹)
25,000	Post office recurring deposit	6.2	9,00,000	9,91,446
25,000	Aggressive hybrid fund	9.5	9,00,000	10,44,851
25,000	Flexi-cap equity fund	12.5	9,00,000	10,96,517

If you need a corpus of ₹10 lakh in three years and you can save ₹25,000/month, where should you put it?

Source: Value Research

In each case, if you commit ₹25,000 per month, which comes to a total commitment of ₹9 lakhs over 36 months, you will come close to the goal. The post office recurring deposit will give you slightly less than ₹10 lakh, while the funds would give quite a lot more. But – and this is a big *but* – the post office deposit is absolutely guaranteed, whereas the funds could undershoot if the market falls. If you *absolutely must have close to ₹10 lakhs* at the end of three years, the post office is where you should park your funds.

Two approaches: Goals or risks

Traditionally, there are two ways of matching portfolios to a client's needs. One, which some investment advisors prefer, is to classify it by specific goals that a portfolio fulfils. For example, funding a college education or house purchase. The second method is by the degree of risk that a portfolio (or rather the portfolio owner) can bear. So, a high-risk, high-return portfolio can be deemed 'aggressive' while one lower down the risk scale can be 'conservative'.

In the following chapters, we suggest four readymade model portfolios that you can use to serve a wide variety of investment requirements. We've taken the second approach, but with a twist. Conventionally, an 'aggressive' or 'conservative' tag is assigned to an investor and applied to their entire holdings. However, our approach is that the two perspectives must be combined. Investors must think of individual needs and then decide which ones need an aggressive approach, and which one conservative.

One easy and accurate way to decide this is by time frame. The shorter the investment period and the more precise the financial requirements, the more conservative you need to be. If an investment is being made for something that is required after seven to ten years, your approach can be very aggressive.

Our aggressive to conservative spectrum incorporates ideas that we have explored earlier. One is that equity is more aggressive than debt. Also, within equity investments, putting your money in relatively smaller companies is a more aggressive approach than investing in larger ones because while smaller businesses can grow faster, they can also run into trouble more easily.

Tracking portfolios

Having a portfolio customized to your needs is not the end of your task. Portfolios must be monitored and tracked because situations change and sometimes, they change very rapidly. Some funds may decline in performance, and you may no longer be on track to meet your goals.

The biggest problem that investors face while monitoring their portfolios is a lack of information and of automated tools to analyse that information. To be able to track various aspects of your investments, you need an easy and automated way of analysing them in detail.

However, this isn't easy for an individual investor to do by themselves.

Value Research provides a set of highly sophisticated, yet completely free web-based tools that help create and monitor portfolios. These tools are built into the 'Portfolio Manager' function on the Value Research website (valueresearchonline.com). To use it, all you have to do is to visit the site and register. Once you have registered, simply click on the 'My Portfolio' or 'My Investments' link to create your portfolio and enter details of the funds (and stocks) that you have invested in. You can create up to five different portfolios to track separate financial goals.

In sum:
- To ensure that you are on the right track to fulfil your goals, portfolios must be monitored regularly and changes made if necessary.
- Value Research provides a free, sophisticated portfolio manager feature on their portal, valueresearchonline.com, that makes it easy to do this.

Here's a list of what you should track along with details of how the Value Research Portfolio Manager will help you do that.

To track	Use feature
Current portfolio value and gains	The 'Overview' tab tells you the latest value of each individual holding as well as the total. This data is updated every evening soon after the fund companies release the day's NAVs. Stocks data is updated by 5.30 p.m.
Returns generated by individual investments. Use this to monitor whether your investments are generating the rate of return that you expect and if any investment is underperforming.	The 'Performance' view provides a detailed analysis of returns. The rupee gains as well as the annualized rate of returns are available for each investment. The total returns and gains are also available for the portfolio as a single entity.
Whether the target asset allocation is holding true. As explained earlier, each of your portfolios should have a target equity and debt percentage. If this balance deviates from what you want, you may need to rebalance your investments.	The 'Analysis' view tells you how much of your money is in debt and how much in equity.
News about the funds you have invested in	The 'Fund News' view on the Funds page has links to news and articles on valueresearchonline.com that may be connected to the funds in which you have invested.

The following chapters have several ready-to-use portfolios that you can use to serve a wide variety of investment requirements. As stated earlier, there are traditionally two ways of matching portfolios and needs.

One is by specific goals and the other by the degree of risk. So a high-risk, high-return portfolio can be aggressive while another one lower down the risk scale can be conservative.

In the portfolios you will see in the next few chapters, we have taken the second approach but with a twist.

Summary

- To ensure that you are on the right track to fulfil your goals, your portfolios must be monitored regularly and changes made if necessary.
- Value Research provides a free, sophisticated Portfolio Manager function on its website that makes monitoring easy and accessible.

8

Types of Funds and Their Uses

There are currently roughly 1,500 mutual funds on offer in India, and these are spread across many categories and subcategories. It's useful to take a quick look and understand how each one works.

One of the major categories is **equity funds**. These can be subdivided into several categories such as index funds, diversified equity funds, small-cap, mid-cap, large-cap and multi-cap funds. The word 'cap' is shorthand for market capitalization (also called market value), which is calculated by multiplying all the outstanding shares of a company by the price per share. In theory, if you bought the entire company, this is what you would pay. Investors divide companies into categories by their market cap and different mutual funds focus on different categories.

A big profitable company will have a correspondingly high market cap while a smaller company will have a low market cap. If a company is profitable and growing quickly, the value of its shares will rise, and so of course, will the market cap.

Simple arithmetic tells you that a small company with low market cap can grow faster than a large company with a high market cap. But a small company also has less resources than a large one, which means it can also run into trouble more often.

Another category is **debt funds**, which deal in fixed-income instruments and specialize in terms of categories and of tenures. Some deal with government debt and some with corporate bonds. Some deal in very short-term instruments, and some deal with long-term and medium-term instruments.

There are also **hybrid funds.** These deal in both equity and debt instruments, and they tend to target holding fixed ratios of each category of assets except for Dynamic Asset Allocation and Balanced Advantage funds, which do not follow fixed ratios.

Tax-savings funds, such as **ELSS**, offer tax benefits and have a minimum lock-in period of three years. These are also equity oriented.

There are some specialized funds which allow Indians to **invest their rupees abroad**. There are quite a few of these to choose from, and they each have differing investment objectives.

You can also buy **sector and thematic funds**, which invest in specific areas, and you can also invest in a **fund of funds**, which holds portfolios consisting of units of mutual funds.

So that's all about categories. We now come to another important question: what specific characteristics of fund types does an investor need to know about and work with?

Different types of funds will fit different investment needs. You need funds that deal in safer, less volatile assets if you're looking for short-term returns. You need funds that deliver a lot of growth to beat inflation if you're looking at long-term funds. There are various shades of in-between.

Equity funds

These are relatively high-risk investments because stock markets can have sharp declines and equally sharp rises. However, stock prices are ultimately linked to economic growth, and India is a growing economy. If you can hold onto an equity fund for an appreciable length of time (at least three years in our opinion and preferably longer), its volatility gets smoothed out. What's more, if you are using an SIP and the market drops, you know that the eventual returns will be higher because the averaged cost of acquisition comes down during the downturn. Equity can give you returns that far exceed anything that a fixed-income instrument can provide.

Within the equity category, you need to understand the different risk-return profiles of subcategories. ***Index funds*** are relatively safe, passive investments. An index fund mirrors the position of the index and a Nifty Index fund will hold the 50 constituent stocks of the Nifty in exactly the same proportions as the index, giving you a market return. In the long term, the stock market index usually outperforms fixed-income instruments. The Nifty's 10-year performance works out to a compounded return of 11.8 per cent. That's well above the 8–9 per cent that fixed income instruments returned in the same period.

Diversified equity flexi-cap funds give the fund manager the flexibility to buy whichever listed stocks they think they'd like to invest in. Thus, there's a higher risk but also higher returns for the funds that have savvy managers who have shown consistent performance. Our analysis at Value Research looks at fund performance over the long term and the five-star funds in this category have consistently returned 15 per cent compounded or better over five-year periods.

Small-cap, mid-cap and large-cap funds are categorized according to the market capitalization of the companies they invest in, but the funds have the flexibility to buy across different industries. For example, a fund might buy into a large-cap IT company or a small-cap IT company or a large-cap auto manufacturer or a small-cap auto manufacturer.

Large caps are safer – big companies are big because they are well-managed, successful businesses. However, large-cap growth rates are lower, and this is partly due to the arithmetic of having a large base. It is also true that when a business has dominant market share in a segment (for instance Maruti in automotives, or ITC in fast-moving consumer goods), it is hard to grow faster than the industry overall. As a result, large-cap returns are relatively lower.

Mid-caps returns are higher than large caps, but there's more risk involved. *Small caps* returns are very volatile, but returns can be very high. In terms of arithmetic, a small company (like Infosys in 1993) can double its revenues every year for several years due to the low base. But smaller companies are more vulnerable to downturns, and so, small-cap share prices can fluctuate alarmingly.

The easy way to remember this is that both the risks and the returns rise as the companies get smaller.

You cannot build growth without an equity component in your investment strategy. But you can be conservative in that you may choose to hold only index funds, large caps or hybrids. Alternatively, you can be aggressive and hold mid-cap and small-cap funds. If you are aggressive, you should get better returns over the long-term but you also have to live with greater risk of losses.

Diversification

This may be a good time to talk about the virtues of diversification. If you only hold shares in a single business, your returns will be subject to volatility due to the cyclical nature of economies. If you hold shares across multiple industries, some of those businesses will be doing well at any given time. And this is the argument for holding diversified equity funds. An index fund gives you this diversification, but index funds track large caps and so the returns may be lower than in a flexi-cap diversified equity fund.

More broadly, the diversification argument also holds across assets. There are times when fixed-income instruments do well, while equity does badly and vice versa. And so, you should have some of both and remember the golden rule: **don't put all your eggs in one basket.**

Efficient markets

The argument for holding index funds that give a return that mirrors the stock market average is fairly straightforward. In an efficient market, where information spreads quickly to everybody and where anybody can trade shares, it is very hard to beat the average return as captured by the index.

Indeed, most diversified equity funds do not consistently outperform the Nifty Index. However, in practice, records indicate that some managers do beat the index return consistently. So there's a case for holding diversified equity funds. But remember that you won't do badly if you only focus on index funds.

Overlap

Let's say you check Value Research's fund ratings while making an investment as millions of people do. You should not blindly buy two of the top five-star funds in the same categories. Take a look at their portfolios and compare their top holdings, and you'll notice a lot of overlap. The best funds in a given category tend to hold the same companies in slightly different weightages. Hence, there's no point in buying two sets of the same stocks. If you notice a high degree of overlap between two fund portfolios, choose one or the other but not both.

Debt funds

Debt funds are safer than equity funds but it's important to know debt funds also carry some risk. Quite apart from the risk of bankruptcy for corporates, there is some risk even in debt funds dealing in government treasuries, which are in themselves totally safe instruments.

The risk comes in because of changes in interest rates, which change all the time. The Reserve Bank of India (RBI) sets policy rates based on where it thinks inflation is headed. The RBI also auctions government debt, and the yields on treasuries reflect inflation and money supply expectations. Commercial banking institutions also take their cue from these rates and set their interest rates accordingly. How interest rate risk works may seem counter-intuitive unless you've thought about the subject.

In the interest of completeness, here's how interest rates are structured. There are many interest rates in a market economy like India. The more risk the lender perceives, the higher the interest rate it will charge. You can skip the detailed explanations in the next few paragraphs and just hold on to that one thought.

The RBI sets what are called 'policy rates' (as do other central banks elsewhere), which it reviews every two months. These are two connected rates – the rate at which the RBI lends money to banks, and the rate at which it borrows money from banks (the processes are more complicated than simple loans but you don't need to know the details). The RBI considers all sorts of variables like inflation, likely future economic growth, the trade balance of imports and exports, the rupee's forex rates, etc., when it reviews monetary policy and resets policy rates.

The policy rates are the foundation of the entire interest rate structure of the economy. Based on those two policy rates, banks lend money to each other at interest rates that are quite close to policy rates. In addition, government debt is auctioned by the RBI and the auction rates are again linked to policy rates. These are all very 'safe' loans in the sense that the government is unlikely to default on its debt, and ditto for banks lending to each other.

Now, based on all these low-risk interest rates, banks and other lenders set commercial interest rates. These include the deposit rates banks pay to borrow your money. They also include the rates at which banks lend money, to retail customers as well as businesses. Based on those rates, credit card companies and micro-finance institutions lend money as well. As the risk of default rises, so does the interest rate.

Credit rating agencies assess the credit profile of a potential borrower. Reliance Industries can borrow ₹20,000 crore a lot cheaper than you can when you take on a personal loan of ₹20,000.

Now consider two situations. Let's say the interest rate on automobile hire purchase goes up. Now, the value of vehicle loans given out earlier at lower interest rates goes down. This means the existing portfolio of a vehicle finance lender is devalued. Now, let's say the interest rate goes down. The value of vehicle loans made previously at a higher interest rate goes up. This means the existing portfolio of lender gains in value.

This is why debt funds, banks and other lenders actually suffer losses when interest rates rise, and they gain when rates fall. Moreover, debt funds (and banks) also trade debt based on their expectations of inflation and rate movements. When they get it wrong, they suffer losses.

Debt funds that deal in very short-term debt ('money market funds' in common parlance and 'overnight and Liquid Funds' in the jargon) are almost immune to these movements, but their returns are not much better than bank deposits. (The money market is the market for very short-term institutional loans or trades in treasury instruments. A bank may borrow money for 24 hours, or a company may raise a 2-day loan. Or some entity may sell a government treasury bill at 97 per cent of the value with an agreement to buy it back for full value, the next day)

Other debt funds give better returns, but they carry more risk while being safer than equity funds. Funds that deal in corporate debt hold the highest risk because companies can default or go bankrupt. But they also give the highest returns. By and large, debt funds are good for protection from inflation and they offer income schemes. They are also useful for situations when you want an SWP. In some circumstances, when interest rates are falling, they can give high returns.

Hybrid funds

As mentioned earlier, these funds have mixed investment objectives. They are very useful for 'conservative growth' since their equity component offers growth while the debt component offers stability. We'll discuss them at length when we talk about model portfolios.

Overseas funds

There are some specialized funds which allow Indians to **invest abroad** in rupees. The advantages to holding these include some of these reasons. There are times when the Indian economy is in a slump while say, the US or Europe is performing well. At this time, overseas exposure will generate growth. Second, these funds offer a hedge against currency volatility. The rupee has fallen substantially versus the dollar in the last few years. An overseas fund invested in US securities is a hedge against such moves. You can also invest in an overseas 'fund of funds' that offers an exposure to several world economies and categories.

Fund of funds

The name of this instrument indicates its purpose. These funds buy units of other mutual funds, thus capturing averaged returns of mutual funds across categories. If you're looking for a very broad exposure, a fund of funds is worth considering.

Sector and thematic funds

There are funds that invest in specific areas. By and large, we would advise avoiding these. The leading companies in a given sector would usually be held in the portfolios of a diversified equity funds in any case.

Now, how do you judge which funds to buy? One good thing about the mutual fund industry is that there's a fair degree of transparency and prompt release of data. But on the other hand, there's a lot of data and it can be confusing. You can try to work through the data yourself, or you can look at websites like valueresearchonline.com which gather the data and analyse it for you. Value Research (and our competitors) calculate not only the returns over different periods but also calculate the risk in terms of volatility of returns. We also analyse and compare fund portfolios.

The ideal investment, of course, is a fund that delivers high returns consistently without great volatility. You should also look at factors like expense ratios (there are ceilings on these) and see whether the fund is sticking to its stated mandate. One point worth noting is that the best funds in a category tend to deliver returns that are fairly close to one another and if Fund A had the best returns in 2021, Fund B may have the best returns in 2022. Thus, it is critical to **look at the long-term returns and ratings not the one-year performance.**

Summary

Here's how you can think of investing in mutual funds:
- Equity funds for growth
- Debt funds for stability of returns
- Overseas funds for currency hedges and multinational company exposure
- Hybrid funds for stability with growth

9

Investing for Growth: Model Portfolios

If you're good at business, the best investment is probably growing and expanding your own business. However, even if you're not good at tackling the real-world problems that any business faces, you can become the part-owner of a business via the stock market. By buying shares, anyone can reap the financial advantages of being a business owner without having to take on all the challenges of running one.

When you boil it down to the basics, you can only do two things with your surplus funds. One, you can store the surplus for safekeeping; and two, you can try to make the surplus grow.

Option 1 can be split into two 'sub-options' – a foolish one and a wise one. The foolish option is to store money in such a way that it loses value because of inflation.

Conversely, the wise option would be to do exactly the opposite thing – to store your money so that the returns stay ahead of inflation. Remember that when we say 'store', we mean putting it in all kinds of fixed deposits, whether it's with a bank or post office, or others. We'll discuss these options later.

However, storing money makes sense only when you know you'll need it for a specific purpose in the short to medium term, within a timeline of perhaps two or three years at the most. If you have savings that you don't need to use for a specific purpose for a relatively short-term period, it's more sensible to try and make your money grow.

Investing for growth inevitably means investing in equity instruments. This may sound like a dogmatic statement, but it's usually the only game in town for most people. However, if you have a talent for selecting art that will appreciate, or you have a deep knowledge of specific commodities, you may be able to find other options. But if you don't have such special skills, and you want real growth, growth that can beat inflation in the long term, then equity is the only option.

To understand why this is so, one needs to understand the source of equity profits. The ultimate source of profits is the growth of the economy. Overall, the stocks of successful businesses grow at rates that are at least equivalent to the growth of the overall economy. Note that when we say that the economy (or the gross domestic product [GDP] or the gross national product [GNP], both of which are measures of the economy) is growing at a given rate, we are speaking of real growth after adjusting for inflation, which is almost inevitable in a growing economy.

The demand for various goods – labour, metals or chocolate as the case may be – is growing and prices go up until such time as the supply of those things rises. This is a benign cycle as long as there's growth, but it does mean that the country will experience inflation. Thus, while this might seem a simplistic way to understand the concept, real GDP growth is always accompanied by some degree of inflation. However, remember that the opposite is not true – there can be inflation without growth.

If inflation is at 5 per cent and the GDP grows at 5 per cent, then, on the whole, stocks will grow at least 10 per cent on average – businesses with products in high demand will grow faster. As an investor, if you can select stocks of businesses that are experiencing high demand and thus, beating the average rate of economic growth, then the returns on your investment can far exceed the rate of economic growth in the country.

Index funds, which mirror the Nifty Index, have given nominal returns of about 11.8 per cent over the last ten years. This reflects the prevailing inflation rate plus the real rate of growth as seen in India's biggest companies between 2013 and 2023. It is much more than the returns from a debt fund. However, **diversified equity mutual funds that are performing well have given returns of anywhere between 15 and 20 per cent compounded over the same period.**

The large returns that a diversified equity fund provides compared to those from an index fund is due to its flexibility of being able to pick and choose its investments (unlike an index fund). Well-managed funds have picked up businesses where growth has outpaced the GDP growth considerably and created wealth for their investors.

The consistently high returns are the basic argument for making long-term investments in equity. No other asset class matches it over such long periods. In contrast, fixed income investing (the storage option) is inherently linked to the inflation rate.

Bear in mind, though, that the returns cited above are averages calculated across listed companies over a long period. There are big variations in returns, not only across individual investments but also variations due to the time under consideration. Shares in a given company might gain 100 per cent in a few months or they might lose a huge amount. The same company could gain or lose a lot during different periods as well.

To ensure that you capture gains from equity:
- Hold your investments for a minimum of three years or longer.
- Hold a diversified portfolio.

When you're setting up a portfolio you need to give due thought to your needs; to the level of risk you are willing to take; to the time period you're going to hold. Given the vast number of available mutual funds, and variations in individual needs and timeframes, it's not possible to exhaustively analyse all the options. One size will not fit all and you have to make your own decisions. But we can suggest some model portfolios as signposts that help to nudge you in the direction you wish to go.

Model portfolios

Let's look at a few model portfolios that investors seeking growth could use. These will give you a sense of how you need to plan. The actual funds you choose may be different, but the characteristics you must look for will be similar to our suggestions. You could pick one of the following profiles

- Stable growth: This type minimizes risks as far as possible, and is most suitable for the investor who

wants growth but doesn't wish to risk losing capital.
- Growth but with some safety: Here, while there is some chance of losing capital, it isn't very high.
- Aggressive growth: For this type of portfolio, the investor is prepared to risk capital for high growth.

The key points to note in each case:
- Time frames. Short time frames equate to taking on less risk.
- Weightage of funds. You will need to mix and match funds of different types in different ratios to get the sort of return and risk profile you want.

Think through your needs and once you've decided on your profile, you can see what we suggest.

Model portfolio: Growth and stability

Time frame: 3+ years

We would suggest a simple portfolio if you're seeking growth with a lot of safety. Pick two or three equity-oriented Aggressive Hybrid funds. These funds typically invest in both debt and equity and in terms of weight, they typically have 70 per cent of their assets in equity and 30 per cent in fixed-income investments. They also automatically rebalance exposure between equity and debt to maintain this ratio.

Model portfolio: growth and stability

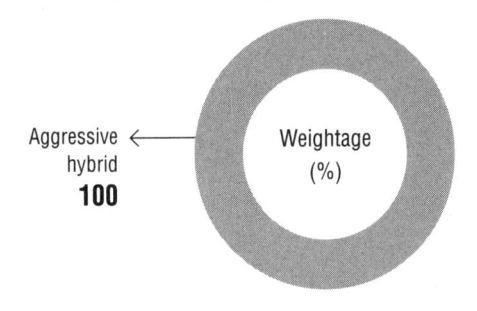

Aggressive hybrid ← Weightage (%)
100

Choice of actual funds
Aggressive hybrid (choose any two to three)

Fund	URL for details
Axis Equity Hybrid	http://vro.in/f37134
DSP Equity & Bond	http://vro.in/f15793
ICICI Prudential Equity & Debt	http://vro.in/f15815
Mirae Asset Hybrid Equity	http://vro.in/f30604
SBI Equity Hybrid	http://vro.in/f204

Source: Value Research

Fixed-income exposure means that your returns are more stable than pure equity funds. Also, automatic rebalancing means that the gains made by the equity components during bullish times are booked as profits and shifted to fixed-income components. Thus, there's protection from losses when stock markets are down.

Despite this, these funds are not immune to market volatility. A 70 per cent weightage of equity is quite a lot and when stocks decline, these funds lose money even though the losses are less than that in pure equity funds.

It is extremely important you do not make lump sum investments in these funds. All investments should be done gradually through an SIP.

Even if you have a lump sum to invest in this portfolio, you should place it in a short-term debt fund and transfer it to the equity funds through an STP.

Model portfolio : High growth (with some safety)

Time frame: 5+ years

A growth portfolio is designed to generate the maximum returns possible from equity investments while somewhat limiting the associated risk. As with an aggressive portfolio, the greatest weightage is given to equity funds. However, in this category, rather than focusing on smaller companies, most investments are made in funds that track large-cap companies with a track record of relatively stable growth for an equity fund.

Even so, you can expect some volatility and when the stock market declines, your portfolio may suffer short-term losses. However, if you hold your investment through the long term, the gains will more than balance out the losses.

As with all equity portfolios, it is very important that you don't make lump sum investments. All investments should be done gradually through an SIP.

Investing for Growth: Model Portfolios

Model portfolio: high growth

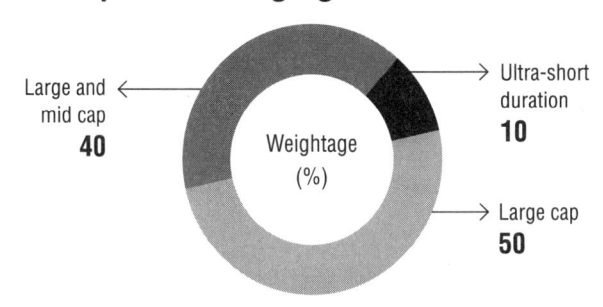

- Large and mid cap: **40**
- Ultra-short duration: **10**
- Large cap: **50**

Weightage (%)

Choice of actual funds

Ultra-short duration (choose any one)

Fund	URL for details
Bandhan Ultra Short Term Fund	http://vro.in/f36956
HDFC Ultra Short Term Fund	http://vro.in/f37806
SBI Magnum Ultra Short Duration Fund	http://vro.in/f16890

Large cap (choose any two and check for overlap)

Fund	URL for details
Axis Bluechip Fund	http://vro.in/f15682
Kotak Bluechip Fund	http://vro.in/f16337
Mirae Asset Large Cap Fund	http://vro.in/f6762
SBI Nifty Index Fund	http://vro.in/f16233
UTI Nifty Next 50 Index Fund	http://vro.in/f36491

Large and mid cap (choose any two and check for overlap)

Fund	URL for details
Invesco India Growth Opportunities Fund	http://vro.in/f16770
Kotak Equity Opportunities Fund	http://vro.in/f16378
Mirae Asset Emerging Bluechip Fund	http://vro.in/f16563

Source: Value Research

Even if you have a lump sum to put into this portfolio, you should place it in an ultra-short-term debt fund and transfer it to the equity funds through STPs. This can be done very easily because this portfolio includes a short-term debt fund.

To build a growth portfolio, look at the weightages recommended for each category and then choose any one or two of the funds under that category.

- If you have a lump sum to invest, park it all in an ultra-short-term debt fund. Retain 10 per cent in the debt fund. Set up STPs to transfers 90 per cent into the chosen equity funds.
- Allocate 50 per cent to large-cap funds
- Allocate 40 per cent to mid-cap funds
- Set up STPs to transfer from the debt fund to the equity funds in 12 equal monthly instalments.

If you don't have a lump sum to invest, decide how much money you want to allocate every month and use the same 50:40:10 ratio.

At its simplest, this portfolio has only three to five funds spread across three categories. Remember to compare portfolios within the equity categories to reduce overlap.

Model portfolio: Aggressive growth

Time frame: 7+ years

An aggressive growth portfolio is designed to get the maximum possible returns. It does this by emphasizing equity investment and within equity, there is a focus on smaller companies. It is intended for an investment target that is seven years or more away.

The portfolio is likely to face a lot of volatility, and its value will likely see sharp falls many times. However, over the long term, the volatility will smoothen out and the gains will more than compensate for it. In this model, 40 per cent of the weight would be given to large caps and mid caps, while 50 per cent would go to small caps and mid caps.

As always, it is extremely important that you do not make lump sum investments. All investments should be done gradually through an SIP.

Even if you have a lump sum to invest in this portfolio, you should place it in a short-term debt fund and transfer from there into the equity funds through STPs. This can be conveniently done because this portfolio includes a short-term debt fund.

To build a growth portfolio, look at the weightage that we have recommended for each category and then choose any one or two of the funds under that category.

Model portfolio: aggressive growth

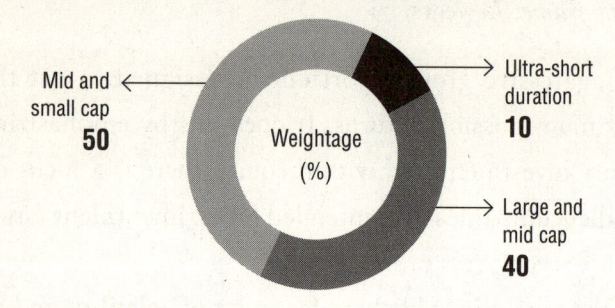

Mid and small cap: **50**
Ultra-short duration: **10**
Large and mid cap: **40**

Weightage (%)

Choice of actual funds

Ultra-short duration (choose any one)

Fund	URL for details
Bandhan Ultra Short Term Fund	http://vro.in/f36956
HDFC Ultra Short Term Fund	http://vro.in/f37806
SBI Magnum Ultra Short Duration Fund	http://vro.in/f16890

Large and mid cap (choose any two and check for overlap)

Fund	URL for details
Invesco India Growth Opportunities Fund	http://vro.in/f16770
Kotak Equity Opportunities Fund	http://vro.in/f16378
Mirae Asset Emerging Bluechip Fund	http://vro.in/f16563

Mid and small cap (choose any two and check for overlap)

Fund	URL for details
Axis Midcap Fund	http://vro.in/f15690
DSP Midcap Fund	http://vro.in/f16438
Kotak Emerging Equity Fund	http://vro.in/f17134
Nippon India Small Cap Fund	http://vro.in/f16182
SBI Small Cap Fund	http://vro.in/f15787

Source: Value Research

Common characteristics and differences in model portfolios.

- Note some of the key factors in the model portfolios:
- The lower risk profiles are allocated to the short term.
- The debt element is higher in the lowest risk portfolio.
- The higher the risk profile, the longer the term of staying invested.
- The highest risk profile has a small-cap focus.
- All the portfolios must be built using SIPs.
- Even the highest risk profile has a debt component.

Summary

- If you're investing for growth you have to accept some risk.
- The higher the targeted return, the more the risk you must take.
- High-risk, high-return portfolios must have long timeframes to smooth out volatility.

10

Using Debt Funds to Invest for Income

In the last chapter, we looked at ways to make your money grow. When you are earning and saving, with the prospect of several decades of continued employment ahead of you, it is the ideal time to invest with the goal of growing your savings. Any volatility that results from ups and downs in the stock market will be smoothed out by time.

However, if you're nearing retirement, you may be looking to generate a regular income from your hard-earned savings rather than aiming for growth. Or, you may want to buy a house on mortgage and let your investments take care of the monthly EMIs. Or, you may be looking at a situation where your 15-year-old child is headed to college in a few years, and you'll need to pay hostel and tuition fees.

These are typical scenarios. In such cases, if you're investing for income, putting your money into stocks is not very suitable. The volatility could hurt you. Instead, you should invest in fixed-income assets such as bonds and deposits issued by companies or banks and in government debt such as treasury bills.

Your portfolio will consist of fixed-income funds or debt funds which are suitable for generating regular income because they have lower risk factors and higher predictability of returns. Since they are safe and predictable, these funds also work when you need to invest for a short period, even if you decide to accumulate the returns instead of withdrawing them regularly. Although debt funds in the same category are quite like each other in terms of returns, they have several subtypes. The differences make them more or less suitable for different purposes.

The sections in this chapter will help you understand debt funds and how to use them.

How debt funds work

Debt funds generate returns by investing in bonds or deposits of various kinds to earn interest. They also trade such instruments, buying and selling debt to each other. An individual can invest directly in some types of debt, but a debt fund has access to far more in terms of assets. Apart from bank deposits, you can buy corporate debentures or tax-rebate bonds and, in theory, even government treasuries. But this is a very cumbersome process and involves making a minimum commitment of large sums at the minimum, and these instruments are not very liquid to boot.

A debt fund can buy all these instruments easily, and they can invest in many types of debt unavailable to individuals. For example, corporates issue commercial paper (unsecured short-term loans) and bonds (legally secured loans), and banks and other financial institutions also borrow from each other. These markets are exclusively institutional. The government of India issues bonds, which are auctioned by the RBI. The government is, in fact, by far the largest borrower in the country, and the Indian bond market is in practice an entirely institutional market.

Most of the bonds discussed in this chapter can be traded on the bond market. The NSE has a bond market section. As explained in chapter 8, the market price of bonds changes if the interest rate changes or if traders anticipate a change in interest rates. If a mutual fund buys a bond and its price rises, then the fund can make more than what it would have from the bond interest income. Obviously, the opposite is also true if the price of the bond falls.

But why do bond prices rise or fall? Let's look at an example. The government of India issues debt through auctions run by the RBI. The auction goes as follows. The government says, 'The Government will give you a demand draft (that is, a Treasury Bill) for ₹100 that can only be cashed 364 days later. How much money will you pay for it now?' Lenders bid for the treasury bill.

Let's say a 364-day treasury bill is auctioned at ₹93.46. This means that the buyer gets a yield of 7 per cent when the government returns the money (Rs 100/93.46 equates to 7 per cent return).

However, the next morning, the RBI decides to cut the interest rate by 0.5 per cent. The treasury bill is now worth more. It can be sold for ₹93.81 because that will be a yield of 6.5 per cent. The buyer can make a profit of 0.35 paisa. This may not seem much, but it works out to a profit of about 0.37 per cent in just one day, which is equivalent to an annualized rate of roughly 135 per cent. If you're dealing in many thousands of crores, that's a terrific return. If, of course, the RBI hikes the interest rate, the opposite occurs and the price of the bond falls.

In general, the value of a bond goes up (or down) if the interest rate falls (or rises).

Bond funds look for trades like this every time there's a change in interest rates, or even if there is the expectation of such a change. Despite the fact that the bond itself may be absolutely safe and risk-free, these trading dynamics can result in big gains or losses for funds that hold bond portfolios. Funds that deal in corporate debt run the additional risks of potential default as well.

Maturity and residual maturity

A bond is defined by two characteristics: the maturity and the credit rating. We've explained how a change of interest rates could make a bond more or less valuable. When interest rates fall, older bonds locked into a higher interest rate are worth more. Conversely, when interest rates rise, older bonds locked into a lower interest rate are worth less.

This rise or fall in value is proportional to how much time is left for the bond to mature and be redeemed with the principal being returned. For example, when interest rates fall, all older, higher-interest bonds gain value. But a bond which has, for example, 10 years to maturity will gain more value than one which has only one year left for maturity. After all, the 10-year bond will go on paying a higher interest rate for much longer.

So bond traders look at residual maturity rather than the total lifetime. Residual maturity mean the amount of time is left till the redemption of the bond. In this sense, a 20-year bond that was issued 18 years ago and a freshly issued 2-year bond have the same residual maturity. If other things about these two bonds are the same, a change of interest rates should impact their value equally.

Thus, the risk and return level of a bond is determined by its residual maturity. The shorter the maturity, the more predictable, the less risky and possibly the less profitable, a bond will be. Longer maturity bonds will show the opposite characteristics. This is why maturity and residual maturity are the most obvious ways to classify bonds, and debt funds are classified as ultra-short term, short term, medium term, etc., depending on the tenures of the bonds they hold.

Special categories

There are some debt funds that focus on special categories of fixed-income assets.

Government securities: Some funds invest only in government securities. These securities, (called gilts), are considered 100 per cent risk-free and are treated like cash by banks and the RBI. This is because they have something called 'sovereign guarantee' – the chance of the government defaulting on loan obligations is very low.

Fixed-maturity plans (FMPs): Many debt funds are open-ended. However, there are also many closed-ended debt funds that are both popular and useful. These FMPs are launched on a specific date for a specific period. Investors must enter them at the launch and remain locked in till the end of the period. Thus, there is low liquidity. However, FMPs offer predictable and high returns with lower risk as compared to open-ended debt funds. The fund can hold bonds of suitable maturity that are either bought directly or off the bond market so that it redeems its holdings at the right moment. It can ignore temporary interest rate changes.

FMPs are considered an excellent alternative to bank fixed deposits. They generally offer higher returns and are considered more tax efficient despite the changes to the Tax Code effective April 2023, which makes them less attractive.

Thus, investments in these categories can offer a range of very useful choices for investors looking for fixed-income options from mutual funds.

Debt funds versus fixed deposits

For most investors, debt funds are a direct alternative to bank fixed deposits. This is a fair comparison as both serve the same purpose in a portfolio. However, there are some differences, and it is important you understand these.

The primary differences are in terms of safety and

taxation (and thus returns) with mutual funds holding a small advantage in tax-adjusted returns and fixed deposits in safety. As with all mutual funds, there are no guarantees in debt funds. Returns are market-linked, and the investor is fully exposed to defaults or any other problems. However, that's a legalistic interpretation of the safety of your investments in debt mutual funds.

In practice, the fund industry is closely regulated and monitored by the regulator, SEBI. Regulations put in place by SEBI keep a tight rein on the risk profile of investments, the concentration of risk that individual funds are facing, how the investments are valued, and how closely the maturity profile adheres to the fund's declared goals.

In the past, these measures have proved to be generally effective, and there have been few defaults by debt funds. Practically speaking, you would be entirely justified in expecting not to face any defaults in debt fund investments. In theory, **banks are safer, but there is no practical difference between the safety level of banks and debt funds** as far as defaults of underlying investments go. However, there's no guarantee for mutual funds, whereas bank deposits are insured up to ₹5 lakh.

The other difference is that of **taxation**. Returns from bank fixed deposits are considered interest income and have to be added to your normal income. The bank usually deducts this every year. If an investor is in the top tax bracket, that's **effectively close to one-third of interest income being deducted.**

As far as debt funds are concerned, **returns are not taxed unless units are redeemed**. From April 2023 (for the financial year 2023–24), interest income from these instruments will be taxed at the normal tax bracket of the investor but only upon redemption – there is no presumptive deduction at source every year. **Another important distinction is that losses incurred on debt funds can be offset against profits from other trades or carried forward to be offset against future profits.**

Using debt funds for income

Investment for income refers to when you need to regularly withdraw a part of your investment to meet living expenses. Generally, this method is used by retired people.

When an investment is made for income rather than for accumulation, many of its characteristics need to be different. First, the returns must be predictable. When money is invested for long-term growth, it doesn't really matter if you get somewhat higher or lower returns at different times during the holding period. It doesn't even matter if you lose money on paper for some of the time as long as there are periods of gain to more than balance out periods of drawdown. However, if you need to make regular withdrawals, uneven returns are not desirable.

Second, this predictable rate of return needs to match the inflation rate, or at least come close to matching it. If it doesn't, your money is just losing value.

Third, the investment needs to be liquid, by which we mean that it should not have a long lock-in period and you should be able to withdraw from it regularly (if required at short notice) without facing any problems or incurring any financial penalty. There aren't too many investment avenues that satisfy all these needs. Investors who are not too knowledgeable generally use a savings bank account for this purpose. These accounts score well on criteria number two and three – they are safe, predictable and highly liquid. However, their interest rate is low, and that's a deal breaker. The interest rate banks offer on savings accounts is never even close to matching the rate of inflation. Lying in your savings account, your money loses real value and buys less and less as time goes by.

If you decide to opt for fixed deposits, these offer a higher rate of return. As banking products, they are safe and predictable, but they obviously score poorly on liquidity. If you need regular monthly income from fixed deposits, then you'll need to set up a cumbersome roster of fixed deposits maturing every month, and that's not a very practical option.

Debt funds are a much better options to fulfil this investment need. The best suited sub-category are short-term debt funds. The returns are fairly predictable, and they also have excellent liquidity – usually you can withdraw your money with one day's notice at any time. In addition, the returns also compare favourably to bank fixed deposits.

Alternative uses for debt funds

While it's true that debt funds are more suited to the purpose of generating income than equity funds, they can also be used for capital appreciation. The difference is that their returns are lower, and their risk (and thus the predictability) levels are higher. This means that they are used for capital appreciation in somewhat different scenarios from equity funds.

Here are some of the uses (apart from income) you can put a debt fund to:

- Stability for an equity portfolio: Equity portfolios benefit from having a small, fixed amount of debt investments because they serve as a cushion against too much volatility as well as a safe holding area for equity profits through asset rebalancing. You will note

that the model growth portfolios suggested in Chapter 9 all have a debt component.
- Opportunistic profits from interest rate movements: This is not a beginners' technique, but it's useful to know about it, and we will discuss this in a later chapter.

Using debt funds to provide stability to an equity portfolio

Debt funds play an important role in an equity portfolio, which is something that many equity investors do not understand. Asset rebalancing is one of the most useful and yet most ignored ideas in the world of investing. While it sounds complex, it's actually very easy to understand, and it's even easier to implement for mutual fund investors.

Asset rebalancing requires investors to view the equity-vs-fixed income situation in shades of grey rather than in black-and-white terms. Based on the time horizons of your separate financial needs and your risk tolerance, you could decide to allot a percentage of your financial investments to equity and some to fixed income. But every so often, once every year or so, you could 'rebalance' your portfolio. What this means that if the actual balance of equity and debt has veered away from your originally desired ratio, you can shift money from one to the other basket in order to return to that percentage again.

When equity is growing faster than fixed income – which is what you expect most of the time – you can periodically sell some equity investments and reinvest in fixed-income instruments so that the balance would be restored. When equity starts lagging, you can periodically sell some of your fixed income and move it into equity.

This rebalancing implements the basic idea of booking profits and investing in the beaten down asset perfectly. Since economies have cycles, things inevitably revert to a mean at some point or the other, and that means equity will start lagging behind debt at some stage. But you have already booked some of the profits you made when equity was riding high and moved them into a safer asset.

The real benefit of this is seen only when the markets start falling and the value of the equity component of a portfolio starts declining. Even though the equity part of this portfolio would fall when the market falls, equity profits that have already been moved into debt funds continue to earn returns. If equity valuations fall a lot, you can move money out of debt and into the stock market at low average cost of acquisition.

Of course, it takes hard work to implement this concept on your own. But balanced funds, which are also called hybrid funds, and which we've recommended several times, can do this automatically for you since their mandate involves maintaining a ratio between assets.

So, what sort of balance should you maintain? We've not discussed this explicitly but the model portfolios we've suggested indicate the sort of balances investors can consider. By and large, if you're young and have several decades of a professional life ahead, you should be aggressive and look for high-growth investments, which means a low debt component. If you're older, you should be more inclined to look for stability of return. And, as we've said before, short-term needs should be catered to by portfolios that offer stable returns.

Here's a model portfolio that a conservative investor who wants safety with a little growth thrown in, could consider.

Model portfolio: conservative growth

Time frame: 1+ years

A conservative growth portfolio allows a high degree of safety, but it still allows the investor to take some advantage of the growth potential of equity. It does this by using a hybrid (balanced) fund, but of a subtype that is much more conservative, and light, on equity than the ones we used for the stable growth portfolio in chapter 9.

Just like the equity-oriented hybrids in that portfolio, these will also implement automatic rebalancing between equity and fixed income and thus protect your returns.

This portfolio has a much smaller degree of volatility than the ones we have seen, but some volatility does exist. As and when the stock markets go down sharply, you can expect some losses.

Ideally, one should invest in this portfolio through an SIP and avoid lump sum investments. However, if you must invest a lump sum, then averaging it over two or three months should be enough.

Choosing your funds is a very simple exercise.

Model portfolio: conservative growth

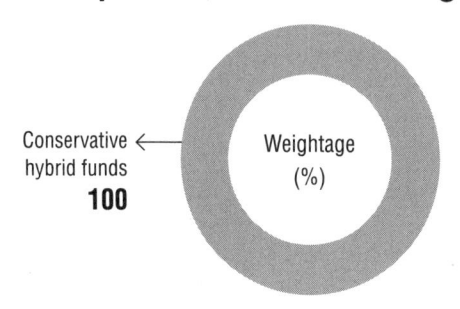

Conservative hybrid funds
100

Weightage (%)

Choice of actual funds
Conservative hybrid funds (choose any two or three)

Fund	URL for details
Canara Robeco Conservative Hybrid	http://vro.in/f15770
HDFC Hybrid Debt	http://vro.in/f16453
ICICI Prudential Regular Savings	http://vro.in/f15851
Kotak Debt Hybrid	http://vro.in/f17795
SBI Conservative Hybrid	http://vro.in/f17516

Source: Value Research

Summary

- Debt funds are safer than equity funds but give lower returns.
- Debt funds are not entirely risk-free. Their value fluctuates with interest rates and residual maturity.
- A debt-oriented balanced fund can offer stability and growth.

11

Long-Term Planning for Retirement

Investing for retirement is a common life situation that every one of us faces. However, it presents some unique problems, which make it quite different from any other type of financial event in terms of planning. For one, it is usually done over an extremely long range, ideally starting decades before you actually retire. Secondly, retirement planning involves both investment as well as disinvestment.

During your working life, you will accumulate money and hopefully, you will grow it. After retirement, you will withdraw your savings and gradually deplete them. **However, even while you withdraw your savings, you must ensure that the remaining amount stays invested and keeps growing at a rate that exceeds inflation by a good margin.**

Think back to your life in the year 2000 and about how many things have changed since then. It's a safe bet that you didn't anticipate many of the technological shifts that have occurred, or the COVID-19 pandemic or the many economic events that have altered our lives in the last 23 years.

In the same way, when you're planning retirement, you're looking into a future just as distant or even more, and there's no way you can predict what the world will be like at that time. Therefore, your planning has to account for both known unknowns and unknown unknowns.

Not only must you start planning for retirement decades before you actually retire, you must also assume that your retired life may be several decades long. And so, if you start planning for retirement when you're in your mid-20s – as you ideally should – you are looking to work out what to do over a period of 60 years. People usually don't understand the maths or realize the implications of making financial plans over such long timeframes.

First, let's deal with a fallacy and explain why we think you need to plan for a really long life. In India, the **average life expectancy at birth is 70 years**. Many people assume that this means a retired person, on average, will pass away soon after ceasing work. But **life expectancy averages are deceptive**. This figure is skewed lower due to a high infant

Long-Term Planning for Retirement

mortality rate and also the relatively high rate at which younger people die of non-natural causes. Close to 2 lakh Indians die every year in road and rail accidents. Those tragedies pull down life expectancy averages because that's just how the maths works.

If you live till 60, your average life expectancy is actually 75 years if you're male and 77 years if you're female. You have, obviously, not died as an infant, and you haven't died in an accident, etc. And this is *still* an average.

If you're part of the urban, middle-class or higher-income population – which is very likely if you're reading this – and you have access to reasonable medical care, **your average life expectancy at 60 is actually 81.** If you cross 80, you're likely to live another 7 years.

This means, again on average, that you will have a post-retirement life of around two decades or more. Many people live well into their 80s, and some live into their 90s. Think about it and you will realize that your life could eventually have a very different trajectory from what you've imagined.

If you live to be 90, then you will have spent 25–28 per cent of your life in childhood and education, 37–40 per cent of it working full-time and around 30 per cent of it in retirement.

Essentially, you must earn enough during those productive years (the 40 per cent of your life you spend

working) to sustain your lifestyle through the next 30 per cent of your life.

You must also assume that inflation will continue to eat into your savings and your healthcare costs will steadily escalate as you grow older.

What you will need to spend in retirement will be far higher in nominal terms than what you needed to spend earlier in your life. And you don't want to face the nightmare of running through your savings and living out your last years in penury.

India doesn't have a social security system and nor does it have free healthcare in practical terms even though 'Right to Health' is a Fundamental Right. The poor standards of a permanently under-funded and under-staffed government health system means that you will end up turning to the private sector, and paying through your nose for private healthcare, unless you were a government employee.

The health insurance industry is also unwilling to provide meaningful coverage to older people who need it the most. If you run out of money, you could be on the street in your old age. If you can't pay for healthcare, assume you won't get it. All this means that the burden of retirement savings weighs very heavily upon us during our working years. However, it is not an impossible burden, provided we start **saving early and invest our savings wisely**.

Accumulating savings for retirement

As a long-term project, you should understand accumulating wealth for retirement is no different from any other long-term savings projects. However, if you talk to conventional financial advisors, you will discover that this approach is considered contrarian. For some reason, a school of advisors believes that because one should not take risks with one's retirement savings, one should not invest them in equity. Or at most, one should invest only a little bit in equity.

This view is not only wrong but dangerous. If you follow it, you are very likely to spend your old age in poverty. This may sound brutal, but it is the plain truth and not an exaggeration.

The general advice about sticking to fixed income deposits of various kinds as the only safe option for retirees because equity is risky is wrong. **In truth, it's not just wrong, it's utterly misguided, and any senior citizen following it is heading for financial disaster.**

Unless you have an independent source of income like rent, which is inherently inflation-adjusted, you are doomed to suffer from poverty in in your old age if you don't protect your savings from inflation. Interest from fixed deposits simply will not keep up with inflation over a long period.

What are the pitfalls if you decide to invest in equity? Let's take a realistic example. Suppose you had retired in 1980 with a kitty of ₹5 lakh that you had invested in a hypothetical investment (such as an index fund) that tracked the Sensex, the index of the 30 top stocks listed on Bombay Stock Exchange.

Let's say that your monthly expenses were then ₹3,000 a month (a very comfortable lifestyle in 1980), and your expenses grew about 10 per cent a year. After 43 years, with compounding, your monthly expenses would be ₹1.8 lakhs, which requires a high net worth to support. But you would have no trouble funding these expenses, since your principal would have grown to ₹26.5 crore!

The Sensex has returned a compounded 16 per cent interest for the last 43 years. But what about the risk, you might ask? During these four decades, the Sensex has faced steep declines several times – in 1987, 1992, 2001, 2008 and 2020 – and it has taken them in its stride comfortably and recovered smoothly to beat inflation by a good measure.

If retirees want to spend their twilight years comfortably, investing in equity is the only hope. Yes,

equity investments are risky but only over short periods of time. Over long periods, equity investments grow, and the real inflation-adjusted purchasing power of fixed-income investments declines.

But the volatility risk of equity becomes more significant as you get close to retirement. That's something you must take note of. You can ignore a market downturn when you're 35 or even 55 years old. You can simply wait for the trend to change. But if the market falls when you're 75, it presents a problem if you're overinvested in equity.

Preparing for retirement

There are some mandatory savings such as provident funds, which are essentially fixed-income instruments. This is not a bad thing since it enforces a discipline that guarantees that you save something. But if you follow our advice, you will put your non-mandatory retirement savings in equity-backed mutual funds, and we suggest you look at something like the model portfolio for aggressive growth suggested in Chapter 9 for one of your portfolios.

When you are five to seven years from retirement, you must start thinking about protecting your savings from the potential volatility of equity. This is crucial for sensible investment planning. A cornerstone of our approach to investments is that all long-term investments should be equity-focused, but an equally integral part of the approach is that when we're getting set to actually utilize the investments, you must protect yourself from the equity risk.

By this logic, if you expect to retire at the age of 62, then by the time you are 55–57, you should start transferring your investments from equity funds to fixed-income assets. However, as we've noted, retirement presents complex problems which can't be tackled in such a simple way.

A retired senior citizen should look to avoid losses in their investment portfolios, and they need to generate an income. But there is a price to be paid for following an ultra-safe strategy. Inflation will just kill your purchasing power in the long run if you switch completely to fixed-income instruments.

The key is to understand what you must do when you retire. **You're still looking to grow your savings and beat inflation for the next 30 years, or longer, but you need to protect some of your savings from equity risks. Therefore, it is imperative your post-retirement investments should still hold substantial equity exposure.**

One way to do this is to use a combination of balanced funds. For example, you could build a portfolio around two types of hybrid funds, held in equal measure. For example, 50 per cent of a portfolio could be equity-oriented Aggressive Hybrid funds. The remaining 50 per cent could go into what we call a debt-oriented Conservative Hybrid fund.

Equity-oriented hybrid funds have around 70 per cent exposure to equity (about 65–80 per cent equity is the mandate) and the rest in debt, while debt-oriented hybrids generally have the reverse ratio of 70 per cent exposure to debt (about 75–90 per cent debt is the mandate) and the rest to equities. Between them, you will still hold 50 per cent of your investment in equities.

As we have suggested in every one of our portfolio suggestions, you should not make any lump sum investments in equity. Make your investments gradually, preferably through an SIP. This is necessary in order to avoid the risk of a sudden market crash that would wipe out a large proportion of your money.

However, this is mostly applicable only if you are making investments in equity from a non-equity source, such as cash or from a fixed-income investment or deposit. When you are transferring money from an all-equity to a partial-equity portfolio, then you are moving down on the risk slope and a faster transfer is not a problem from the risk perspective. So you could move lump sums out of equity into balanced funds without incurring a large risk of volatility.

Either way, at least a couple of years before you retire,

you should start to transfer some equity assets into fixed income. This will set you up nicely for a long, stress-free retirement.

Model portfolio: income and retirement

Time frame: Not relevant

Unlike all our other portfolio suggestions, this one is designed not to put money into savings but to take it out. However, just like the others, it is designed to grow returns and tries to ensure that what you take out doesn't deplete the real value of what remains. The portfolio is designed for a withdrawal rate about 8 per cent per annum.

However, since there is a strong equity component in it, this is an average rate. There could be times when it's better to withdraw a little less. As such, this is not a portfolio which is necessarily useful for a guaranteed monthly income. All the funds in here are hybrid funds. Half of them are equity-centric Aggressive Hybrids and half are debt-centric Conservative Hybrids. Overall, the equity exposure of the portfolio is about 50 per cent.

Again, like any portfolio with equity, when money is placed into the portfolio, it is extremely important that you don't make lump sum investments and make them gradually through an SIP. Even if you have a lump sum to invest in this portfolio, you should place it in a short-

Model portfolio: income & retirement

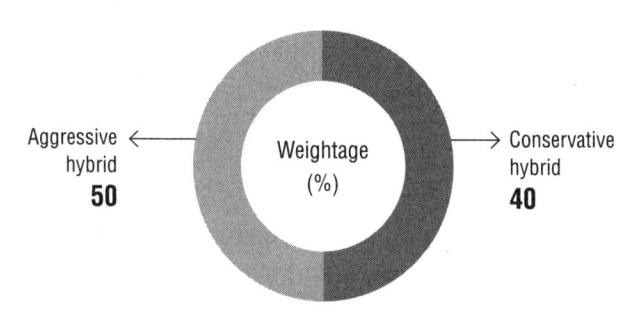

Aggressive hybrid **50** ← Weightage (%) → Conservative hybrid **40**

Choice of actual funds

Conservative hybrid (choose any two)

Fund	URL for details
Canara Robeco Conservative Hybrid	http://vro.in/f15770
HDFC Hybrid Debt	http://vro.in/f16453
ICICI Prudential Regular Savings	http://vro.in/f15851
Kotak Debt Hybrid	http://vro.in/f17795
SBI Conservative Hybrid	http://vro.in/f17516

Aggressive hybrid (choose any two)

Fund	URL for details
Axis Equity Hybrid	http://vro.in/f37134
DSP Equity & Bond	http://vro.in/f15793
ICICI Prudential Equity & Debt	http://vro.in/f15815
Mirae Asset Hybrid Equity	http://vro.in/f30604
SBI Equity Hybrid	http://vro.in/f204

Source: Value Research

term debt fund and transfer it to the equity funds through an STP.

Research the weightages we have recommended for each category and then choose any one or two of the funds under that category.

Income and growth after retirement

Earning a regular income from investments after you retire is one of the most vexing problems in personal finance. On the face of it, this shouldn't be the case because post-retirement income is not an unusual investment requirement – in fact, it is possibly the most common need for most people. Every financial advisor or consultant has some sort of a recipe to recommend to clients for a post-retirement portfolio.

Unfortunately, much of this advice is suboptimal. Invariably, its starting point is that retirees cannot risk anything except fixed-income options like debt funds or different kinds of deposits because any option that includes equity is too risky. As we've said earlier in this chapter, this is not just wrong, it's utterly misguided and any senior citizen following this will head for financial disaster.

Retirement is hopefully going to be a long period of your life. If you retire at 60 or 62 and then live to your mid-80s, that's over 20 years and you should plan for longer. Logic says that post-retirement planning involves ensuring an income stream as well as planning to invest your savings to beat inflation for another 25–30 years without taking on any high risk.

What does that mean while constructing a portfolio? As we have said earlier, the balance of equity versus fixed income in your asset allocation should not be decided by how old you are, or some other measure of risk-taking ability. Instead, **it should be governed by how long you are investing for.**

Money that you would not need for more than five to seven years is best left in equity funds. There will be ups and downs, but the downs will be amply compensated for by periods of strong growth.

Retirement-oriented mandatory savings

Even though equity is the best way to make long-term investments for retirement, many people have already had that choice somewhat limited or taken away. Retirement-oriented savings that are part of our employment profile are almost entirely based on fixed income.

This is true for both government and for private employees. The Provident Fund (PF) – both the individual Public PF (PPF) and Employees PF (EPF) version –

yields fixed income as far as you are concerned. The EPF of course is mandatory for employees and the PPF a very popular instrument since it offers a tax break.

But while PF assets may be invested anywhere and have an actual return of anything, this is not your concern. You are receiving a fixed rate of return guaranteed by the government. Even newer options like the New Pension System (NPS), which have been introduced in the last few years, are based on fixed-income investments.

The NPS was conceptualized to allow substantial equity exposure in some of its plans. The NPS, as it has been implemented as a mandatory scheme for government employees, has a ratio of 90 per cent fixed income and 10 per cent equity. But in Tier 1 up to 75 per cent equity is allowed, and in Tier 2 100 per cent equity is allowed.

The one distinctive thing about mandatory requirements is that the employer generally matches the employee's contribution. As a result, the returns effectively double. Therefore, in that sense, the mandatory amount you have to contribute to the EPF is a good investment. It ensures that you save something in a disciplined manner even though the returns are low and will not match inflation in the long term. However, it does not necessarily make sense to invest any extra money that will not be matched by the employer.

Most readers will be familiar with the contours of the EPF, the PPF and the NPS. But in the interests of completeness, a quick summary of the features of these retirement schemes follows.

New Pension System (NPS)

1. The returns are not guaranteed but there is a government assurance that a minimum assured return will be offered. As of the time of writing (May 2023), this has not been announced so we have no details.
2. The costs involved include:
   - One-time account opening and issuance of a permanent retirement account number (PRAN): ₹40
   - Initial subscriber registration and contribution upload: ₹200–400
   - Annual maintenance charges: ₹69
   - Each transaction or deposit: ₹3.75 + 0.5 per cent of contribution (min ₹30, max ₹25,000)
   - Annual custodian charge: 0.0032 per cent of the fund value
   - Annual fund management charge: 0.03–0.09 per cent of the fund value
3. The minimum investment involved is:
   - Initial contribution along with the subscription application: ₹500

- Maximum deposit in cash: ₹25,000 per transaction
- Minimum amount to be deposited annually: ₹1,000

Public Provident Fund (PPF)

1. The investment required for PPF is:
   - Minimum investment: ₹500 per annum
   - Maximum investment: ₹1,50,000 per annum
   - Deposit frequency: No maximum limit
2. The returns on a PPF investment are:
   - Annual rate: 7.1 per cent compounded annually; this rate is reviewed every quarter.
   - Calculation: The interest for the month is calculated on the minimum balance available in the account from the fifth of a month to the last date of the month.
3. The conditions of the tenure of a PPF investment are:
   - Lock-in period: You must be invested for 15 years.
   - On the completion of the lock-in: Your PPF account can be extended in tranches of five years until you wish to withdraw your money.
   - Maturity tenure: A PPF account matures after 15 years, but the contribution has to be made for 16 years in all. The 15-year period is calculated from the financial year following the date on which

the account is opened. Hence, the PPF account effectively matures on the first day of the 17th year.
- The capital invested in the PPF is guaranteed. However, the mandated rate of return may not match inflation – in fact, there are long periods when it does not. Even though the return is tax-free, the very long holding period makes it very likely that inflation will eat into the value of the amount.

Taxation for senior citizens

As you would have gathered by now, we strongly believe that inflation is the greatest threat to a happy retirement. The ideal situation would be to have a source of income which is inherently inflation-adjusted. And it's not impossible to arrange in the course of your working life – in fact, many retirees have such sources, the most common source of which is rent, which can be raised gradually to match inflation.

However, investments tend to be the dominant source of income for retirees. But with income comes the issue of income tax. There are some tax exemptions available for senior citizens and older citizens pay less tax. Moreover, if the bulk of their income is derived from investments, there are other ways of getting a lower tax liability. Here are some easily usable ones.

The most useful thing is that long-term capital gains from equity funds and equity-oriented hybrid funds are much lower than the tax slab applicable if you are in the highest tax bracket. If you hold an investment in an equity fund for over 12 months, your tax incidence of profits are defined as long-term capital gains. The tax applicable is 10 per cent, which is one-third of the highest income tax bracket. Moreover, any losses incurred can be carried forward to be offset against future gains.

In fact, apart from agricultural income, long-term capital gains from equity-based investments is the only legal way to reduce tax on income in India. However, if you derive income from equity-oriented hybrid funds, this income must come in the form of long-term capital gains. Therefore, it should be derived from selling units of the fund, taking care that there are enough units that have been held for over a year.

Another tax-saving option is to withdraw up to ₹1.5 lakh a year from taxable mutual funds and invest this amount in an ELSS. Up to that limit, an ELSS held for its three-year lock-in period is effectively tax-free. If you need more complex tax saving solutions, you should consult a tax expert.

Summary

- You will need to undertake retirement planning for 50–60 years.
- Assume you will live 25–30 years post your retirement.
- The only way to beat inflation is by using equity investments.
- While you can seek safety by holding a larger fixed-income component, you must keep a large equity component to beat inflation even after retirement.
- Check with an expert for effective tax-saving strategies.

12

Exchange-Traded Funds, Insurance and Unit-Linked Insurance Plans

There are some instruments which are very similar to mutual funds but with some very different individual characteristics. They pool the savings of individuals with investment decisions being taken by professionals.

One important instrument is the exchange-traded fund or ETF. ETFs are just like a mutual fund, in that they have units that are traded on stock exchanges just like normal shares. They mostly track stock indices or specific assets. Some ETFs hold gold and silver for instance, and there are ETFs that track the Nifty. Some offer overseas coverage and track stocks listed on the Nasdaq Index or the New York Stock Exchange (NYSE). There are ETFs that track other stock indices such as the Nifty Auto index or the Nifty Private Banks index.

The market price of an ETF should, in theory, reflect

the price of its underlying asset, whatever that is. Since these funds are listed on various exchanges, they are quite liquid and offer very wide coverage of assets that are otherwise not easily available.

For example, an investor using rupees can get exposure to overseas companies such as the digital giants FAANG – Facebook (now Meta), Apple, Amazon, Netflix and Google (now Alphabet) via the Mirae Asset FAANG ETF. Apart from benefiting if the share prices of these companies go up, this ETF offers easy currency protection since it gains if the US dollar strengthens against the rupee. On a broader front, exposure to the Nasdaq-100, an index of the biggest listed Nasdaq stocks, is available. The indices of other stock markets such as Hong Kong (Hang Seng index) can also be accessed using this method.

An ETF is also a convenient way to hold assets like gold and silver electronically rather than hoarding bulky physical ingots or jewellery. There are many precious metal ETFs listed on the NSE, which generate a lot of trading volume. An ETF is also a convenient way to have exposure to debt instruments, such as government securities, or to the liquid money market (which includes short-term loans by financial institutions to each other). It can also be a useful way to get sector exposure in segments like private banks, healthcare, automobiles and auto ancillaries if you desire this sort of narrow exposure.

Some or most of these assets are also available via mutual funds, but the expense ratios for ETFs are better. Gold ETFs are popular and so are overseas stock ETFs. Sovereign gold bonds offer the same coverage for gold, and you could get a better deal from the sovereign bonds. But if you wish to hold some silver, you may have to go with an ETF since it is the most convenient option unless you are comfortable directly trading in the commodity futures markets or storing large quantities physically.

However, there is one downside to buying and holding an ETF. It is invariably priced at a discount to the underlying asset or basket of assets. Another way of understanding this is that an ETF is always at a discount to the NAV. If you don't mind this, an ETF is a useful instrument and sometimes, the one-click convenience of trading these supersedes the fact that they will be discounted to NAV. It is good to keep in mind that the discounts are generally stable. That is, a specific ETF tends to always trade at, for example, 10 per cent below the NAV. So, the arithmetic may be that you are buying an ETF at a given discount and selling it later at the same discount. Hence, it may be argued that the discounts usually cancel out.

ETFs can therefore be useful in terms of getting exposure to certain classes of assets. The high liquidity and broad coverage compensates for the discounts.

Insurance

Products offered by insurance companies are often the weakest link in the personal finance affairs of most Indians. Most investors don't understand how insurance works for them and end up holding insurance products which are sub-optimal in terms of coverage, or outright sinkholes for their hard-earned cash. This is not the fault of the saver, but of the government (or rather specifically of the insurance regulator, IRDA), and insurance companies and insurance agents.

Life insurance

For many years, the life insurance business in India was basically a scam. These companies focused on products designed to make the customer poorer by siphoning off huge chunks of the premium payments into the companies' pockets and as commissions to the agents selling the policies. For years, since the 1960s, in many widely sold insurance products, this 'chunk' of commissions was in excess of 80 to 90 per cent for the first few years of the policy. There were even products where it was 100 per cent commission in the first year!

In India, it's quite difficult to make good choices while buying insurance. The reason is that the economic incentives given to sellers make it logical for them to avoid selling you term insurance. The commission is lower where the agent is concerned, and the insurer gets less premium as well. Due to this attitude of profit maximization on the part of the insurance industry, Indians have always been confused by insurance and bad at making the right decisions about coverage.

The most basic rules for taking out insurance, ones that are never taught to us, are as follows:

- Insurance is not investment. Don't confuse the two objectives.
- Insurance is what your family gets if you die and that's all it is.
- If a life insurance policy offers to make your 'investment' grow, then it's not a policy or it's a bad policy.

Think of this way. Insurance is a bet you want to lose. If a policy pays off, your family has already suffered a tragedy. Don't try to make money off your premium. The only approach to buying insurance that is good for your financial health and your families' future prospects is this one.

Step 1. Decide how much money your family will need if you suddenly die: A good rule of thumb is account for 10 years' income, but there could be other factors to think of. For example, you may own a house, or you may have an outstanding mortgage. Consider what income your spouse or other family members have and how many dependents you have.

Step 2. Buy low-cost term insurance that will pay out 25–50 per cent more than the amount you've calculated in Step 1 if the policy has to be claimed: To avoid putting all your eggs in one basket, split your term insurance policies across two companies. As time goes by, your income will increase. Keep reviewing the insurance amount and enhance it to reflect changing needs if necessary. At some point, the need could become static, or decline, as dependents become independent. And once you've made the calculations, avoid agents and just buy online term insurance directly from the company.

A term policy involves a single annual payment. The policyholder gets nothing back. If the policyholder dies, the nominee(s) can claim the agreed amount. Term plans are by far, the cheapest type of life insurance policy. While every insurer offers term policies because they must by law, they try to dissuade people from opting for these. They also provide policies which offer 'money back' or some other form of return after a certain number of years. These are always at nearly zero interest. They also offer market-linked policies called ULIPs which we'll discuss later in this chapter. All those types of policies involve considerably larger premiums for the same cover as compared to term policies.

Health insurance

Buying health insurance is not as straightforward as it should be. The biggest issue is to ensure that the policy will cover every kind of healthcare cost you could face, and you should have adequate coverage. Good medical care is very expensive, and it's easy to underestimate how much money will be needed for medical issues.

Indian health insurance is actually not health insurance but 'hospitalization insurance'. Generally, it's difficult to get a cover for treatments that don't require hospitalization. This can be a big problem because even expensive treatments for life-threatening diseases may be done on an outpatient basis. For example, some cancers require chemotherapy costing lakhs of rupees but don't need the patient to be admitted to a hospital. During the initial phases of the pandemic, cost recovery for COVID-19 treatment at home, involving oxygen cylinders, nursing, etc., was not available for many people. Moreover, health insurance is very expensive if you're a senior citizen since insurers hike the premiums with age.

You should keep these factors in mind while choosing

a health policy. Unfortunately, India doesn't have a social security blanket, and free healthcare of any acceptable standard is impossible to get. unlike in many European countries. In practice, assume that your healthcare costs will escalate steeply as you grow older.

Unit linked insurance plans

You may be wondering why a primer on mutual funds has a section about insurance. Well, insurers offer products called **unit linked insurance plans** (ULIPs) with policies that offer a combination of an insurance cover (meaning a pay out to the family if you die) and an investment structured like a mutual fund with units. These plans invest the premiums in the stock market or in debt, and every insurance agent will try to sell you a ULIP instead of a term plan.

In the ULIP format, a part of the premium goes towards providing the investor with a life insurance cover. The rest is pooled and invested in debt or equity instruments or a combination of both to create wealth in the long term. However, these have some inherent problems that you should consider.

The first issue with a ULIP is that a fairly high commission is taken upfront by the agent and the insurer

– the charges are far more than a mutual fund where expense ratio is strictly controlled. Second, ULIPs tend to have confusing fine print, and you may discover that the insurance cover is inadequate for your needs or structured in an unsatisfactory fashion.

In one sense, ULIPs and mutual funds dealing in the same assets are similar. But you get less bang for your buck with a ULIP than you would if you split up the same amount, took out a term policy and invested the rest in mutual funds. The chances are, this redistribution of funds would buy you more units and get you the same, or more, in the way of insurance cover than the ULIP. Note that there is also less flexibility with an ULIP, which involves lump sum payments, than with a fund where you can use an SIP.

ULIPs also have long lock-in periods of five years or more. The maximum lock-in for a mutual fund is three years for an ELSS, and open-ended mutual funds don't have lock-ins. Mutual funds are more transparent in our opinion – they must release information by the law. Earlier, ULIPs were tax free, but now the tax treatment is roughly the same as mutual funds so the long lock-in makes them unattractive.

Summary

- Ignore the insurance agents.
- Work out what sort of cover you need and take out a term policy to provide it.
- Park any surplus in mutual funds rather than look at ULIPs.

13

Tax Treatments of Investments

There's an old saying about the only two things in life that are unavoidable are death and taxes. Both are, of course, unpleasant subjects to discuss, and we've dealt with death and its implications at length in our sections on insurance and retirement.

So let's talk about taxes. Income tax is a very complex subject, and it cannot be tackled holistically since that would require a separate book with many subsections. Moreover, the Tax Code changes every year with the Budget released by the Ministry of Finance and any specifics may be subject to changes. Our goal is to familiarize you with the taxation applicable to any income or losses that you may have from your investments and the means available to structure your investments efficiently to reduce the tax you have to pay. We will try to give you an understanding of the concepts, but we cannot describe all the details that might be needed to actually file returns.

Paying taxes on investments

Of the various types of investments discussed in this book, mutual funds and stocks are defined as **capital assets,** and the gains from the purchase and sale of these are called **capital gains**. If you lose money on them, then those are **capital losses. Capital gains or losses occur only when you actually sell an investment and receive the money.**

Dividends paid by funds or shares is dividend income, while interest earned from bank, post office or other such deposits is called interest income. Indian tax law treats capital gains and income differently. Here's an overview of the taxation situation of each.

Capital gains from mutual funds and shares:

Type of investment	Holding of less than one year	Holding of more than one year
Shares, equity funds and equity-oriented hybrid funds (in which more than 65 per cent of the assets are equity)	Taxed as short-term capital gains at 15 per cent.	Taxed at 10 per cent

All other funds	Added to other income and taxed as income, according to the investor's tax slab, if held for less than 36 months	Taxed as long-term capital gains, which may be indexed and adjusted for inflation if held for over 36 months

Dividend income from mutual funds and shares:

Type of investment	Dividend tax
All funds	Taxed as income according to the investor's tax slab

Inflation adjustment for long-term capital gains

Tax payers have a choice of two rates at which they pay long-term capital gains for debt funds. You can either pay 10 per cent tax on the gains, or you can pay 20 per cent adjusted for inflation. The inflation adjustment is done according to a calculation released by the tax authorities. If you have held the fund for a long period, especially when there was high inflation, the indexation could reduce your tax incidence. Your chartered accountant will do the calculation and advise you. For investments made in debt funds on or after 1 April 2023, gains are treated as short term and taxed as per applicable slab rates.

Interest income

Interest income is simply added to your income and taxed according to whatever tax bracket you are in.

Saving taxes through investments

Some sections of the Indian income tax law allow you save tax by making specific financial investments. Let's look at some of these.

Section 80C

Section 80C offers a wide window of investment opportunities of up to ₹1.5 lakh in each financial year. This benefit is available to everyone, irrespective of income levels. For instance, if you are in the highest tax bracket of 30 per cent, an investment of ₹1.5 lakh under this section can save you ₹50,000 each year (plus surcharge, etc.).

Various financial products that qualify for Section 80C benefits include:
- Premium payments for life insurance
- Home loan principal repayments, wherein the principal portion of a home loan equated monthly installment, or EMI, qualifies for deduction under Section 80C

- Your contribution to the EPF. The employers' contribution is not deductible.
- Tuition fees upto a maximum of ₹1.5 lakh for upto two children
- Contributions to the PPF
- Investments in the citizens savings' scheme
- Savings in notified term deposits in scheduled banks with a minimum period of five years under the Bank Term Deposit Scheme, 2006
- Savings in post office deposits with a five-year lock-in
- National Savings Certificates, a government-backed security with a six-year lock-in
- Investments in ELSS
- Investments in pension plans

Section 80CCG, or the Rajiv Gandhi Equity Savings Scheme

The Rajiv Gandhi Equity Savings Scheme (RGESS) is a very complex scheme that provides one-time tax relief to new equity investors. If you have never invested before, and your annual income is less than ₹12 lakhs, you may be eligible. The tax relief is not large, and the details are too complex to list here. Check with your chartered accountant if you meet the criteria for investment.

Section 80CCF

Investment in infrastructure bonds up to ₹20,000 per year qualify for deductions under this section. The interest income on these bonds is taxed, but the sum invested may be deducted. That is, let's say you have a taxable income of ₹1 lakh and you invest ₹10,000 in these bonds at an interest rate of 5.5 per cent. After deducting that ₹10,000, you will have a taxable income of ₹90,000. However, when you receive the ₹550 of interest, (this will be in the next fiscal year) it will be added to your income for that year and you will be taxed.

Leave it to your CA

If you're feeling confused about the fine print cited in this chapter, do not worry, you are not alone. Tax laws are indeed complex and confusing, and the tax provisions also change from year to year. We've provided a basic overview of the situation as of the financial year 2023–24 (1 April 2023 to 31 March 2024).

If you're a senior citizen, you will also receive certain benefits in terms of tax incidence which you should avail of. Please explore all the options with a chartered accountant if you are on the verge of retirement and will cross the age of 60 soon.

Summary

- Capital gains are generally taxed at a lower rate than income.
- A long-term gain has lower tax incidence than a short-term one.
- Check with a tax professional to find ways to minimize your tax liability.

14

Picking a Fund: What to Look For

If you have come this far into this book, you should by now have a sense of the basics of investing in mutual funds and some insight into the practical aspects and logic of long-term investing. Hopefully, you've worked out your own investment needs and have a sense of the sort of investment portfolios you'd like to build to fulfil those needs with the least hassle and risk.

As the examples throughout the book should have hammered home, we believe long-term investments should be equity oriented. You now understand how inflation can destroy your purchasing power in the long term unless you find ways to generate returns that beat it. You also know why you shouldn't mix insurance and investing, and you have a sense of the broader tax structures in India.

In addition, you also know something about how to protect yourself from inflation. You understand the utility of asset allocation across equity and debt, and the diversification within equity across sectors and across large and small caps. You've realized that planning for retirement needs to start more or less the instant you receive your first salary. You've also realized that retirement planning never stops – it continues, more or less, until the day you pass away.

If you've absorbed the concept of compounding and understand the power of long-term compounding, you are now convinced that investing in equity for the long term can make you rich. Indeed, it can make you very rich if you can pick the right mix for your portfolio and stick to these investments for the long term. What's more, you don't need to spend a great deal of time managing portfolios if you use mutual funds. You can set up your SIPs and relax and focus on living your daily life. The market will automatically increase the value of your investments.

While it's great that you have all this knowledge, but how do you pick a mutual fund? What are the things you look at when you decide that Fund A is better suited to your needs than Fund B? Let's explore this question in a little depth. Or rather, let us explain why we haven't placed much emphasis on answering this question.

Notice that we've focused on asset allocation and on understanding your needs rather than on the details of picking a specific fund. We've talked about the need to set a ratio between equity and debt; we've talked about using an SIP and explained why rebalancing is useful. But we have not told you that Fund A is the perfect fund for you to target. And we've mostly discouraged you from making direct equity investments.

This is because your asset allocation is much more important than the specific fund or the specific stock you pick. You need to decide what weight equity and debt will each have in your portfolio. If you do that carefully, you could then narrow down to a shortlist of about six funds which meet your investment needs and then throw a die to pick the specific fund. You'll still get a more than acceptable return whatever it throws up.

Basic criteria for picking a fund

There are some basic criteria that you must look for in any given fund. You want expense ratios that are on the low side of the legally permissible, consistent performance and funds that stick to their investment mandate.

Low expense ratios are driven partly by competition, and the mutual fund industry is highly competitive. Expenses ratios are also monitored by SEBI, which allows a maximum of 2.25 per cent of the assets under management (AUM) for equity schemes with the limit sliding down to a max 1.05 per cent if the AUM are above

₹50,000 crore. Debt funds have lower limits, but SEBI would like to reduce expense ratios even further, and it has proposed that fund houses should charge uniform expense ratios.

It's easy to understand the concept of funds sticking to their investment categories. If a fund claims to be large cap, it should hold 80 per cent of its AUM in large caps, A hybrid fund should set 65:35 ratios favouring equity over debt if it is equity-oriented and vice-versa if its debt-oriented.

You want the funds you pick to stick to their category – you don't want to take on small cap risk when you've picked a fund that is ostensibly large cap. There are lots of categories and sub-categories, especially in debt funds – you'll be able to find all the details on websites like Value Research and the Association of Mutual Funds of India.

Finally, there's performance. Funds have benchmarks that their returns are compared to. A large-cap equity fund, for instance, will use the Nifty Index as its benchmark. You want the active funds you've picked to beat the index that is its benchmark over the long term.

If you've invested in an index fund or an index ETF, you want a return that is very close to the index that it mirrors. The difference between the fund's returns and the index's returns is called the tracking error, and this is a key number with an index fund or ETF. You'll find a few funds in every active category that beat their benchmarks in the long term – this will narrow down your shortlist. In the index category, look for the lowest expenses ratios and the least tracking error.

At this point, once you've identified performance, you need to examine risk. There are multiple ways to measure risk. There's the volatility of return, for example. Let's say Fund A consistently returns 15 per cent per annum, while Fund B returns 35 per cent one year and minus 15 per cent in the next and continues to ride this roller coaster. While these two funds may have similar long-term performances, Fund A is less likely to affect your blood pressure because it doesn't suffer big drawdowns. **Make no mistake – any equity fund will have a bad year every so often.** But the smoother the rate of returns, the less the risk to you. You should also remember that the concentration of your portfolio can lead to another kind of risk. If the fund holds relatively few stocks, it may have a more volatile performance.

Websites like Value Research and our competitors look at all those numbers and classify funds. Five-star funds according to us meet all these criteria, and they are leaders in their category. You could just simply look at those rankings and pick these, but in the long run, it helps if you do read the methodology of the fund and understand it. This way, if the fund's performance changes, you have a better sense of what's going on.

However, once you have narrowed it down to the top performers in a category, you can actually can toss a coin if it boils down to making a choice between the top three. One-year performances boil down to a matter of luck with the top funds swapping positions quite often. There may not also be much to choose between these funds when it comes to five-year returns. You don't need to take on undue stress to work out small differences in returns – those will even out in the long term.

You do, however, need to check for overlaps. If two high-performance funds have the same portfolio (or the same top holdings), there is not much point in holding both. Pick one and find another fund which has a somewhat different portfolio.

Averaging by SIP

Throughout this book, we've talked about investing through SIPs. There are multiple reasons to do so, and we've covered them all. But this is an important enough aspect to emphasize again. An SIP gets you an **averaged cost price**. If the market falls for one month or six months in a row, your cost to acquire these units also falls. This gives you a better return in future. Of course, if the market continues to rise, you're getting a good return anyway!

Apart from this simple arithmetic, there are two other factors you must understand. An SIP imposes **discipline** – most of us earn on a monthly basis and we need to invest our surpluses on a monthly basis. SIPs ensure we do that. If you do pick up a lump sum (perhaps a work bonus or an inheritance), you should invest it in an SIP by putting the money into a debt fund and arranging an SWP, which transfers it to an equity fund gradually.

The third reason is that SIPs **prevent us from trying to time the market.** Every so often, you'll hear a lot of noise about the market on TV shows, and it will be a topic of discussion in your friends' circle. Your friends will brag about how they've made a killing or be bemoaning their losses. You will be tempted to follow the herd at those times. By committing your money, a SIP ensures that you don't do this. You can just ignore the noise and let your investments grow.

Should you invest directly in equity anyway?

A lot of people commit to mutual funds and also invest directly. There's nothing wrong with this. Indeed, Value Research and our competitors regularly recommend stocks which appear worthy of direct investment. But this takes a fair amount of time – you must do your own research, and you need to be able to accept a higher degree of risk and volatility if you are investing directly in equity.

Do you have time to spare for in-depth research along with surplus funds? Are you sure you won't get obsessed with stock market fluctuations to the exclusion of normal daily work and life? These are questions you need to ask yourself.

If you have the time and the surplus funds after meeting your basic hierarchy of needs and building a fund portfolio, invest directly by all means.

There are a few things that you must keep in mind for direct investments. **Keep an eye on asset allocation.** You don't want your fixed income plans to skew down to almost nothing because you're making huge commitments in direct equity.

Check if the stocks you wish to buy aren't already in your fund portfolios. If they are, think hard about why you want extra exposure.

Think of direct investment as a tertiary activity:
- Meet your basic needs.
- Build a fund-based investment portfolio.
- Use surpluses to invest directly.

Using debt funds opportunistically

Making money from direct equity investment or losing it is easy to understand intuitively: the price of a stock goes up or down. That's the **risk of equity.**

But **bond fund risks** are harder to understand. We are now going to describe a strategy that only seasoned investment professionals use. It's a fairly advanced approach, and we're including it mostly for the sake of providing a complete picture. If you've reached this far in book and absorbed what we've written, you are clearly not a beginner, or at least, you have the desire to learn.

As we explained earlier, the interest paid is not the only source of income for debt funds. Most bonds are also traded in a debt market, just as equity shares are traded on the stock market. Like anything traded on a market, the price of each bond can rise as well as fall. When the price of a bond rises, that means additional gains for the mutual funds holding that bond. The opposite is true when the price falls.

As you also know, bond prices change in response to **a change in interest rates or the expectation of such a change**. Let's assume that there's a bond that pays interest at a rate of 9 per cent. Then, the interest rates in the economy fall, and newer bonds start being issued at 8 per cent. Obviously, the old bond is now worth more than before. Mutual funds that hold it find their holdings are worth more, and they can make additional profits by selling this bond rather than holding it till maturity and simply enjoying the interest income. Again, obviously, the reverse could happen when interest rates rise. Such a situation may result in some losses for a bond fund. Indeed, if you track stock market prices, you'll notice that banks and other lenders see a fall in their share prices when interest rates rise. This occurs for the same reason.

The amount of rise or fall in NAV is proportionate to what is called the residual maturity of a debt fund portfolio. An instrument, which is scheduled to pay interest for a longer tenure, will be worth more and vice versa.

So, what does it mean to use debt funds opportunistically? People try to anticipate forthcoming changes in interest rates and buy or sell funds that will benefit from these changes. RBI's Monetary Policy Committee meets six times a year to review interest rates.

In the last 12 months, the RBI has raised interest rates to combat high inflation. This is usually a dampener for equity– higher inflation means higher raw material costs for businesses; higher interest rates mean higher borrowing costs; and when things become more expensive, consumers also tend to cut back on purchases.

At some stage, the RBI will lower interest rates again. As and when that happens, the funds that hold bonds (especially government bonds) of long residual maturity will make good gains, and traders will bet on this.

We're not advising you to play this market. **We're suggesting that you be braced for sudden bursts of volatility in the NAVs of debt funds every time the Monetary Policy Committee has a meeting.**

Value Research has multiple free tools which help you to filter and search our database for funds that meet your specific needs and criteria. You can screen for funds according to your criteria, and you can also compare funds and calculate SIPs. The website has examples and explanations on how to use all these tools.

Summary

- Pick funds with good returns, high consistency of return and long track records.
- Look for low expense ratios and avoid portfolio overlaps.
- Use SIPs for investing discipline and cost averaging.
- Invest directly in equity only if you have surpluses after meeting long-term goals.

15

How to Do It: The Nuts and Bolts

There are several ways in which you can invest in mutual funds. Depending on the level of assistance you need, different methods may be more or less suitable for your needs.

In the broadest terms, the two options for investments are, first, making them directly and, second, making them through an intermediary. There are different types of intermediaries available, but the real choice is between these two options. Direct investments result in a higher workload for you, but they yield a significantly higher level of returns. In addition, doing it yourself is faster and more flexible in the sense that you can quickly make changes to the parameters online. If you are digitally savvy, we'd advise you to take this route.

To begin with, you'll need to do a Know Your Customer (KYC) check, the mandatory process of identifying and verifying a person's identity when they are opening an account or even occasionally over the time that they hold an account. If you have a smartphone and a Permanent Account Number (PAN) card and an Aadhaar number , this is a 10-minute process online. Otherwise, it involves filling in a form and handing it over to an AMC, which is not particularly difficult either. The industry body, the Association of Mutual Funds of India (AMFI) has the contact details of AMC offices and of agents sorted by location available on their website.

Then, once you've worked out your needs and decided on the types of portfolios you want, you'll need to pick a selection of funds. While Value Research's tools can help you do this, you can also do it yourself by researching the categories of funds you're interested in on the internet. Many of the links will lead back to Value Research, but of course, we have competitors too! Don't worry too much about picking only the top fund in each category – the rankings change every year and blindly picking any of the top five funds in a category will give you roughly the same long-term returns.

We recommend that you should speak to your chartered accountant or a tax adviser to get a sense of what is the most tax-efficient investment for you. Again, this is not too difficult for most individuals. It's a question of understanding the difference between income tax and capital gains tax and checking if you are eligible for any specific age-related (or other) tax breaks.

You can also ask an investment agent for advice, and this is a double-edged option. The agent will save you some trouble if you're looking to do the investment physically. They will bring you the forms, tell you where to sign and deposit them, etc. They will also give you advice. Of course, they will charge a commission for this and, as we'll explain later in this chapter, this commission could make a significantly negative difference to your returns in the long term. In addition, remember that the agent's advice will tend to be skewed by their relationships with various AMCs and the types of commission they earn.

Incidentally, you need not overly worry about fraud. Mutual funds take money only from your bank account (via cheque, the Unified Payments Interface (UPI), debit card, and direct debits once you've set up a SIP, etc.) and in case of redemptions, they return cash directly to your bank account. If your smartphone is stolen or your bank account is somehow hacked, you may be vulnerable. But the agent cannot run away with your money, though there have been occurrences of this in the past.

Setting up your nominees is mandatory so that if you pass away, your heirs will automatically get access to the units. You can set up multiple nominees and assign a percentage to each, but you must set up at least one nominee. **Ensure you have the nominee's correct name, a contact number or email, their PAN and perhaps their Aadhaar details since you will have to provide these**.

When you subscribe to a fund, the AMC assigns you a unique folio number. This is like a bank account and like a bank account, you have multiple folios with different AMCs. The folio is linked to other financial information (such as your PAN), and even if you forget about your holdings (it does happen!) the databases will not forget! If you are using SIPs, as we suggest, you will need to give your bank a mandate for regular transfers. Again, this is easily done online.

Here, in some detail, are the nuts and bolts of how to invest.

1. **Direct plan:** These have been available since January 2013 when SEBI made it compulsory for AMCs to offer direct plans for every fund. These are now available for all funds, whether they were launched before 2013 or after.

    In the direct route, you have the opportunity to earn a slightly higher return from your mutual fund, even from the same portfolio. **Direct plans do not charge annual recurring commissions, resulting in these plans having lower annual charges, and eventually a higher NAV, compared to regular plans. The expense ratio on a direct plan could be anywhere** between 0.30 and 1 percentage point lower than a regular plan.

Over time, as your money compounds, this difference becomes significant and it's in your favour. **For example, take a look at the HDFC Flexi Cap Fund. In the 10 years since Direct Plans became available, the Direct Plan has delivered a return of 16.46 per cent compounded while the Regular Plan has delivered 15.63 per cent compounded. Say, an investor took an SIP of ₹10,000 per month, committing a total of ₹12 lakh of her savings. The Regular Plan has grown that to an impressive ₹26.71 lakh whereas the Direct Plan has returned an even higher ₹27.87 lakh. The difference of ₹1.16 lakhs is about 4.3 per cent extra return for the Direct Plan. You can switch from regular plan to direct plan, but you have to ask for this – it is not in the AMC's interest to tell you.**

2. **Intermediaries:** There are a wide variety of intermediaries including banks, stockbrokers (including online brokers), individual agents (known as independent financial advisors) and small financial advisory companies. All intermediaries have to be registered with the AMFI, which also maintains a searchable online directory at www.amfiindia.

com. **In order to protect investors, the website also lists intermediaries who have been suspended for malpractices.**

As mentioned earlier in this chapter, the intermediary helps you fill in application forms and submit them and any other documents to the AMC's office. They even bring back purchase acknowledgements. But all these services come for a fee. **Those fees come out of your savings and hence aren't actually invested for you.** Even though the fees are not very large, as the comparison of the Direct versus Regular Plans above will show, it will impact your long-term returns.

In case you hold a Regular Plan, you can convert it to a Direct Plan. However, while this is an instant process, it counts as a redemption followed by re-investment. So there is an expense involved in the switch. Nevertheless, if you intend to continue investing in that fund for the long-term, it is worthwhile doing it.

3. **Directly with the AMC:** You can invest in a mutual fund scheme by investing directly through an AMC. You can do this online, and if you have the requisite documents for online KYC, the process is especially quick. You can also go to the AMC's office and fill

up physical forms. Once you have registered with an AMC, future investments in different funds from the same AMC can be made online or offline using the unique folio number issued in your name. Some AMCs may extend the facility of sending an agent to help you fill the application form, collect the cheque and give you an acknowledgement.

Remember, you have to ask for the Direct Plan and ensure you are registered on Direct Plan even if you are doing it all yourself. In case you're confused, anybody can apply for either the Direct Plan or Regular Plan on their own, or through an intermediary, such as the online broker Zerodha.

However, the default option that will be presented in most cases to an investor is the Regular Plan so you will have to change that option to Direct online, or check the right boxes if you're doing it physically. An individual agent may also charge you a small sum for helping with the paperwork, or walking you through it online, in case you need the assistance.

4. **Online portals:** There are many third-party online portals using which you can invest in various mutual funds. Most investment portals have tie-ups with banks to facilitate easy fund transfer at the time of investing. They charge an initial fee to set up an

account and facilitate future online access to invest and redeem your investments.

5. **Banks**: Most banks are also intermediaries who distribute fund schemes from different AMCs. You can inquire at your bank branch about fund schemes that you wish to invest in. **Remember to do your research first. Your bank will try to sell you schemes that suit them and not necessarily the schemes that earn you the best returns.**

6. **Demat and online trading account**: If you have a demat account, you can buy and sell mutual funds schemes directly through this account. The rest of the process is seamless and the units (and folio number, etc.) will be reflected in your demat account.

So should you go the direct or indirect route?

There are many pros and cons to each route but what you need to remember is:
- Investing directly means eliminating intermediaries and earning higher returns because more of your savings go into your investments. So do this, if you're confident about your choices.
- If you go through an advisor, you are likely to get

investment advice as well as help with the modalities. However, the quality of that advice may vary. Always look at the track record of the schemes that are recommended. Value Research (and our competitors) offer you a free snapshot of long-term performance as well as tools like SIP calculators, and a look at fund portfolios. You can move seamlessly from checking out our investment advice to the AMC or the intermediary of your choice.

Summary

- If you are digitally savvy, you can pick a fund and invest in it very quickly online.
- If you need advice and you want help with the modalities, there are many intermediaries you can pick from.
- We suggest you pick the direct plans – in the long term, not paying recurring charges or agent commissions will boost your returns significantly.

Afterword

If you've come this far with this book, you've learned a lot. Let's do a quick recap of the main concepts.
- You know how to set your hierarchy of needs and how to target those methodically.
- You understand the poisonous impact of inflation on your savings and the need to beat it.
- You understand the need for multiple portfolios to fulfil your specific needs.
- You know how to mix and match debt and equity to create stability and growth.
- You understand the power of compounding and how it can make you wealthy.
- You understand systematic investing and the discipline it brings to wealth creation.
- You have learnt to think for the long term and how to think very long term for retirement.
- You understand how to weigh risk and reward.

It's now up to you to put all this knowledge into practice. This is not actually difficult if you use mutual funds in the ways we've suggested. You can set up multiple portfolios and automate your SIPs with a few clicks of your mouse. After that, it will take no more than an hour of your time every month, at the very most, to ensure things are running smoothly. You can focus on your job or your hobbies and sleep soundly without worrying about the future.

That would fulfil one of the goals of this book. We wish to enable people who are not inherently interested in the world of finance to manage their own money without being either bored by devoting too much time to it or being overwhelmed by the complexity.

People who are bored sometimes end up doing disastrous things with their money to entertain themselves. They obsessively watch TV programmes aimed at day traders, and they focus on every little uptick and downturn in their portfolios. They spend more on brokerage commissions than they make on their trades. People who are overwhelmed by the complexity often end up doing nothing or blindly follow tips, which is just as bad.

You can use the power of compounding to grow your wealth without either having to understand financial complexity or having to devote time that you would rather use to do something else. So long as you understand compounding and you have the patience to let it happen, you can pick a set of mutual funds, set up SIPs and get on with your life.

In addition, if you are interested in finance, there's lots more to learn. Here's a suggestion in case you're interested in learning more. Once you've met your hierarchy of needs and set up your long-term fund portfolios, set aside some surplus as 'mad money'. This should be a relatively small sum of money you don't mind spending on entertainment. You could use this to go on a fancy holiday, buy a high-end home theatre system, or play poker with it. Or you could delve deeper into direct investing and learn how to find winners in the stock market or how to opportunistically trade commodity futures or profit from interest-rate movements. You may lose some money, but you can think of that as the price of tuition or the cost of pursuing a hobby.

You could learn this art on your own or you could check out the Value Research website. We also offer stock investing suggestions, and unlike TV channel gurus who just give tips, we explain the underlying logic of all our recommendations. If you have a flair for it, direct stock investing is definitely a wealth booster.

Whether you decide to take your investing journey a step further or not, if you've absorbed this book, you've learned enough to take charge of your own finances and manage your investments in a way that will result in a steady accumulation of wealth. And we're always there to assist you with any information you might need.

As the Star Trek greeting goes, 'Live long and prosper'!

Acknowledgements

Although this book carries my name alone as its author, it was actually made possible only through the contribution and inspiration from many others.

First and foremost, my readers. This book did not arise in a vacuum – it grew out of literally decades of interacting with investors, listening to their problems, thinking about them and offering solutions. If those people had not got in touch with their savings and investment problems, I doubt if I could have developed and sharpened my understanding of investment.

I would also like to extend my deepest gratitude to the extraordinary teams Value Research has had over the years. The Value Research teams have put together the tech and data, and done outstanding research and analysis, striving over the years to make our work in these areas the best there is. Like everything else connected to Value Research, this book is an edifice that stands on the bedrock of the hard work of all those individuals.

Their dedication, knowledge and ability to dive deep into the mysteries of investing is inspiring. They provided not only their expert knowledge but also their time in making this book comprehensive, insightful and educative. Without their contributions, this book would simply not have been written, let alone reached the breadth and depth it boasts today.

Further, I must extend my gratitude to my friends and family who showed endless patience and offered their unwavering support throughout this journey.

Thank you all!

A Note on the Author

Dhirendra Kumar is the founder and CEO of Value Research, India's leading independent mutual fund information provider. He founded Value Research immediately after graduating in 1990 from Delhi University.

Over thirty-plus years, he has gained a unique perspective by closely observing the Indian mutual fund industry and by interacting with and helping thousands of investors. He is also a popular columnist and commentator in print and electronic media, with regular appearances in leading newspapers and TV channels.

Dhirendra is the chief editor of Value Research's website www.valueresearchonline.com, and its two monthly magazines, *Mutual Fund Insight* and *Wealth Insight*. He is also a member of the Primary Market and Data advisory committee of SEBI and a member of the PFRDA advisory committee, the regulatory body of the National Pension System.

* TIME IS OUR CURRENCY * BOOK 4 KIDS 8-12

GOAL SETTING ↓ 24-1-2?
ABOUT MY LIFE

1) What are your 5 basic values in life? HUMILITY - GRATITUDE - HONESTY - KINDNESS - HUMOUR

2) Ur 3 most important goals in life right now? ①SHELTER 4 US + LOVED ONES
② GROW IN FAITH, WISDOM HUMILITY WITH AGE
③ LEAVE WORLD BETTER OFF + HEALED AFTER

3) What would U do, how wud U spend Ur time if U only had 6mths to live? Spend Time with Mum, Dad, Cuckoo

4) IF U became an instant millionaire what wud U do differently than 2day take away mum + dads health worries, give them the best care, + prepare 4 our Future too (Cuckoo + Me).

5) What Hv U always wanted 2 do but been afraid 2 attempt?
Create smiles 4 children that need it 4 bring them to Jesus like in Don Boscos dream.

6) What sort of activities in life give U the greatest (importance) (feeling of)
Spending time with Cuckoo, mum, dad and praying. and being good to ppl/making them happy

7) What 1 great thing Wud U dare 2 dream if U cud Not Fail? Bring Every 1 I love + care about to heaven with me. Amen

- Things are neither good nor bad, they just are.
- I can feel the stress flowing out of me as I slow down and focus on my breath.
- I can get through anything with the help of my higher power.
- ~~Which~~ With each breath, I let go of my stress.
- I will overcome the stressful situation.
- As I turn toward that higher power, whatever that higher power may be, my anxiety turns to **patience**